Completely Nuts

Completely Nuts

A COOKBOOK AND CULTURAL HISTORY OF THE WORLD'S MOST POPULAR NUTS

MARY MACPHERSON

Doubleday Canada Limited

Canadian Cataloguing in Publication Data

MacPherson, Mary
Completely nuts

Includes index.
ISBN 0-385-25495-4

1. Cookery (Nuts). I. Title.

TX814.M33 1995 641.6'45 C94-932710-7

Design by Avril Orloff
Cover illustration by Sylvie Deronzier
Printed and bound in the USA

Published in Canada by
Doubleday Canada Limited
105 Bond Street
Toronto, Ontario
M5B 1Y3

Contents

Acknowledgments

I wish to thank the following people who so generously shared ideas and information, viewed my project with such enthusiasm and sustained me with wonderful gifts of nuts: Adult Peanut Butter Lovers' Fan Club, Tifton, GA; Blue Diamond, Almond Plaza, Sacramento, CA; Byrd's Hoot Owl Pecan Ranch, Butler MO; Doug Campbell, Campberry Farm, Niagara-on-the-Lake, Ont.; Michael Kelley, Chestnut Hill Orchards, Inc., Austin, TX; Hawaiian Macadamia Plantations Inc., Honokaa, HI; Hazelnut Marketing Board, Portland, OR; Kernal Peanuts, Vittoria, Ont.; Lucas and Barbara Nersesians, Luke's Almond Acres, Reedley, CA; The Maples Fruit Farm, Chewsville, MD; Mellingers, Inc. North Lima, OH; Donna Hammons, Missouri Dandy Pantry; Annie Clark-Bhagwandin, Northwest Chestnuts, Morton WA; Oklahoma Peanut Commission, Madill OK; Peanut Butter and Nut Processors Association, Potomac, MD; Picard Peanuts, Windham Centre, Ont.; Squire's Choice, Langhorne, PA.

I would also like to thank and acknowledge the following people and their recipes: Phylis Bishop, Lemon Walnut Loaf; Byrd's Pecans, Casserole Potatoes au Gratin, Sawdust Pie; California Almond Growers Exchange, Thai Salmon with Almonds; Oliver Saucy, Cafe Maxx, Macadamia-Crusted Snapper, Deep Dish Double Chocolate Chip Bourbon Pecan Pie; Chestnut Hills Orchards, Traditional Chestnut Soup, Spinach, Mushroom and Chestnut Casserole; Joan Colebourne, Viennese Apple-Almond Torte; Toby

Tyler, Electric City Gardens,Chocolate Pecan Sauce; Embassy Suites Hotel, Coconut Chicken Fingers; Elaine Geleziunas, Linguine with Pine Nuts, Bacon and Sun-Dried Tomatoes; Hazelnut Marketing Board, Hazelnut Cream Cheese Brownies, Hazelnut Blue Cheese Dressing, Hazelnut Satay, Hazelnut Mushroom Sauce; Margaret MacPherson, Princess Elizabeth Cake; Mai-Kai Restaurant, Chicken and Cashews; Nancy McCallum, Romesco Sauce; Northwest Chestnuts, Annie Clark-Bhagwandin, *The Chestnut Cookbook,* Walnut-Stuffed Acorn Squash, Mar Hi Gai, Chestnut Tenderloin with Fruit Mingle; Oklahoma Peanut Commission, Peanut Butter Muffins, Peanut Torte; Conrad Croteau, Parkhill Cafe, Basque Chicken; Scaramouche, Fusilli With Seared Shrimp in Coconut Milk Curry; Shoalwater Restaurant, Goat Cheese and Walnut Crackers; Joan Sullivan, Homemade Nuts and Bolts.

Introduction

At any cocktail party people approach a bowl of mixed nuts like birds at a feeder, with an eye to selectively picking away at their favorites. Perhaps what struck me most while researching *Completely Nuts* is just how individual every nut is, which makes me question the wisdom of mixed nut bowls.

There is something unique about every nut — the pistachio is the only nut processed in its shell; the macadamia has no skin at all; the cashew is encased in a toxic resin; and historically, more acorns have been consumed than wheat!

Botanically, nuts are single-seeded, dry fruit. They develop from the ovary of the flower, and are always encased in a hard, woody shell. True nuts grow on trees, although the term "nut" is applied loosely to other edible kernels such as peanuts, a member of the legume family, and seeds, such as almonds and coconuts.

With the possible exception of eggs, nature packages no other food as perfectly as the nut. Consider the walnut, housed like a tiny brain with two kernels on each side. Did you know the halves are identical?

Although nuts are still enjoyed in North America, cereals and other grains have displaced nuts in popularity. Chestnut producers, recognizing the almost equal food value of chestnuts to grains, are making attempts through increased cultivation to re-establish the tree that once represented 25 percent of America's eastern hardwood forest.

Almonds are still California's largest food export, and the sixth largest U.S. food export. And nearly 50 percent of all peanuts, one of

the United States' six basic crops, are consumed in the form of the North American phenomenon: peanut butter.

Nuts have been a part of the human diet since the days of food-gathering societies. But over the millennia the status of nuts has changed, running the gamut between dietary staple and luxury food. In the tropics and Third World countries, both coconuts and peanuts continue to be dietary staples, mostly because grains are not cultivated there.

In Europe, nuts figured prominently in ancient and medieval cookery. The almond, for example, was an essential nut since milk made from crushed nuts could be substituted for cows' milk on Christian fasting days. During Victorian and Edwardian times, nuts were a popular ritual at the end of any "civilized" meal. In France, almonds, hazelnuts, walnuts and chestnuts are taken very seriously; French nut lovers prefer their nuts green or unripe, and most can even distinguish between varietals.

The most expensive, gourmet nuts are pine nuts, pistachios and, macadamias. Compared to other nuts, macadamias have grown in popularity faster than any other nut, since the nut was only officially (botanically) recognized in 1856.

Today, nuts are still an important part of festive occasions, especially Thanksgiving and Christmas, where mixed nuts in the shell appear in beautiful bowls, more often as a centerpiece than a food, but mysteriously vanish by January. No food is as versatile as the nut, nor as well known. This book celebrates the suitability of nuts in every course from appetizer to dessert.

I do believe I've served my last bowl of mixed nuts!

Mary MacPherson

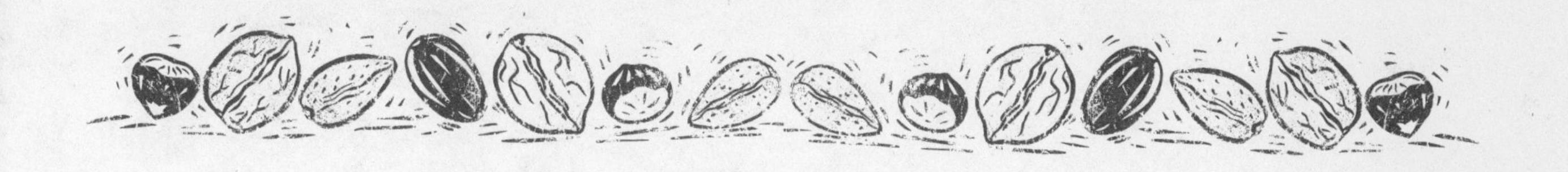

THE Nuts

Almond

The almond is the most commerically important nut available in the world. Prized for its magnificent, sweet flavor — who can resist the taste of marzipan, nougat or macaroon? — and versatility in cooking, more almonds are cultivated worldwide than any other nut, and each year almond acreage is increased to keep up with growing market demand.

The origin of the almond is obscure, but it's believed to have been native to the temperate desert parts of south western Asia, spreading westward to the warm, dry areas of the Mediterranean basin. In 200 B.C., the almond was brought to Italy by Marcus Porcius Cato; he referred to it as the "Greek nut." Cultivation of almonds spread from Greece and Italy to north Africa, Spain, Portugal and France, where in 812 A.D. Charlemagne, King of the Franks, ordered almond trees planted on the imperial farms.

In medieval cookery, the almond and its milk were a significant and popular ingredient. A fourteenth-century cookbook, the *Form of Cury*, written by King Richard III's master chefs, contained recipes for Creme of Almand, Grewel of Almand and Cawdel of Almand Mylke, a soup made with almond milk, ground almonds, onions, wine and species. One of the oldest desserts, *blancmange*, was created by the French in Languedoc, a former province of France. In the Middle Ages *blancmange* was made with sweet and a few bitter almonds, then pounded, pressed and sweetened with honey. A jelling agent made from grated stag horn was eventually replaced by beef or

GENUS: Prunus dulcis

FAMILY: Rosaceae

In southern Europe, almonds are a symbol of good luck. They are still candied and given as a symbol of long life and happiness at Greek, Italian and Czech weddings.

mutton juice and finally gelatin. The dessert was difficult to make; it had to be white and exceptionally smooth.

In North America, almonds weren't cultivated until the eighteenth century. In 1769, when establishing missions between San Diego and Santa Barbara, Spanish Franciscan fathers planted almonds from seed; however, their efforts were unsuccessful as the area was too damp. Around the mid-1800s, areas near north-central California proved more suitable for cultivating almonds.

Initially, almonds were difficult to grow. They had to be planted on slopes and pruned faithfully, as sunlight had to reach every part of the tree. With the improvement of almond varieties, growing techniques and equipment, California now produces about 70 percent of the world's annual harvest, with Spain and Italy yielding about 20 percent.

Almonds are California's largest food export, and the sixth largest U.S. food export. Most almonds are produced in a 400-mile (640 km) stretch between Bakersfield and Red Bluff California.

Sacramento, California, is home to Blue Diamond, the world's biggest almond factory, which comprises 33 city blocks on 90 acres (36 hectares). Over 2 million pounds (908,000 kg) of almonds are processed daily. Almond shells supply the only bio-mass congeneration plant of its kind, providing energy for Blue Diamond and over 10,000 Californian homes.

There are two kinds of almonds: sweet and bitter. The sweet almond is used in the confectionary industry and as a dessert nut. Bitter almonds, while easier and cheaper to raise, contain lethal hydrocyanic acid, which is removed by heating the nuts. Once processed, they are used to flavor extracts, liqueurs and orgeat syrup. It is illegal in North America to sell bitter almonds for human consumption.

The almond tree, unlike other nut trees, is a member of the botanical family *Rosaceae*, related to the peach, plum and apricot. The

A year in which there are plenty of almonds and dates increase prosperity and life.

ARAB PROVERB

Almonds are unique in that their lightly fragrant blossoms open before the leaves do. This phenomenon was noted as early as 300 B.C. by Theophrastus.

In biblical times, Hebrews looked upon the almond tree as a symbol of haste because of its sudden blossoming.

latin name, *Prunus dulcis*, means "sweet plum tree". Resembling a peach tree in appearance, the almond grows somewhat larger, lives longer, but is less hardy than the peach. Sometimes this tree is grown in zones that won't yield nuts simply because it's so attractive.

Most almond trees must be cross-pollinated. Commercial growers plant other varieties with the main crop for that purpose and bee hives are placed among the trees to assure pollination. Gardeners should plant more than one tree, preferably of another compatible variety.

The nuts do not drop to the ground like other ripe fruit, and must be harvested mechanically or by hand once all the hulls have split open along suture lines to reveal the nut. This phenomenon starts on the outside branches of the tree and moves inward.Once gathered, the nuts are then hulled and dried mechanically to a moisture content of less than 8 percent, cleaned, graded, sorted and inspected to determine whether they will be blanched, roasted, shredded, chopped, slivered, diced, split or refined in another fashion. If long-term storage is required, the nuts are fumigated and stored at less than 40° F (3° C).

For the most part, almonds are used dried, when they are richer in proteins, sugar, fats and vitamins. They're especially popular as an ingredient or garnish on entrées. Almond afficianados believe, however, that the nuts are best eaten "green" or not fully ripe.

Marzipan, the sweetmeat made from ground almonds, sugar and unbeaten egg whites, is a confection especially popular at Christmas. This pliable mixture can be formed into shapes like animals and fruits, or rolled into sheets to cover cakes. The name comes from the Italian *marzipane*, which means a sweet box. Almond paste differs from marzipan in that paste contains more almonds and is therefore more expensive. There is more sugar in marzipan, which makes it stiffer and lighter in color than the paste.

With many a bud if flowering almonds bloom,
And arch their gay festoons that breathe perfume,
So shall thy harvest like profusion yield,
And cloudless suns mature the fertile fields.

VIRGIL

The Mohammedans associated almond flowers with hope since the blossoms appear on bare branches before the leaves.

Almonds were considered to be a remedy for drunkenness during the time of Pliny (23–79 A.D.) and Plutarch (46–120 A.D.). In 1579 Gerard wrote in his Herball ". . . that five or six [bitter almonds] being taken during fasting do keepe a man from being drunke."

Marzipan was perfected by the nuns of the French Ursuline order. The fame of their sweetmeats made in a pastry shop in Issoudun was known from the Tuilleries to the Russian court, savored by Napoleon III and Pope Pius IX.

Almond Tree

- **VARIETIES:** *Hall (Kansas and Plains states); Nonpareil, Mission, Carmel (California)*
- **SIZE:** *25–40 feet (8–13 m)*
- **AVERAGE LIFE SPAN:** *50 years*
- **BEARS:** *3rd to 4th year*
- **MATURE YIELD:** *At 7–8 years, 10–20 pounds (5–10 kg) per tree.*
- **CLIMATE:** *USDA zones 6–9; limited to the great inland valley of California, southern California western areas of Washington and Oregon; hardy varieties in Kansas and Plains states; as hardy as a peach, the almonds are at risk, not the trees.*
- **WHEN TO PLANT:** *February/March (west); spring (other areas).*
- **PLANT:** *In deep, well-drained loam or sandy loam.*
- **SPECIAL REQUIREMENTS:** *Frost-free March (when the tree blossoms), and frost-free April (when the nut is immature); long summers of dry heat.*
- **HARVEST SEASON:** *Late summer after husks split.*

COMMERCIAL AVAILABILITY: *Blanched or skins on: whole, broken, cross cut, halved, natural splits, cube cut, diced, chopped, slivered, flaked; roasted; candied; smoked; ground; powder; paste (flavored and plain).*

SELECT: *Unshelled almonds, uniform in size, free of any sign of worm holes. Shelled nuts should be crisp.*

STORE: *Will keep for months refrigerated in tightly sealed containers.*

TO TOAST: *Spread almonds in one layer on a baking sheet; bake until brown at 300° F (150° C) stirring often.*

NUTRITIONAL VALUE: *Almonds are an excellent source of Vitamin E and magnesium. They contain iron, calcium, phosphorous, potassium, vitamins B1 and B2, are high in unsaturated fat and fibre.*

Like to an Almond tree mounted hye
On top of greene Selinis all alone
With blossoms brave bedecked daintily.

FAERIE QUEENE
EDMUND SPENCER
i, 7, 32

Brazil nut

GENUS: Bertholletia excelsa

FAMILY: Lecythidaceae

The largest nut in any bowl of mixed nuts is always the Brazil nut. Just as familiar for its three-sided shape as its size, the Brazil nut is also known as the butternut, *castana, castanea,* creamnut and Paránut.

The Brazil nut is the seed of a giant evergreen tree indigenous to the Amazon forest in South America. It also grows in Central America but is most common in Brazil and Paraguay. Wild stands of Brazil nut trees tower above the rest of the jungle at 100 to 150 feet (33 to 50 m), scattered over one and a quarter million square miles (2 million square km) of the Amazon Basin. The trunks, which can be between 4 and 8 feet (1.5 and 2.5 m) in diameter, grow tall and straight, clear of branches, which only occur at the crown of the tree.

From October until March, beautiful clusters of creamy, white blossoms flower, while the previous year's nut crop is still on the tree. New fruit won't mature for fourteen months after blossoming occurs. From January to June the seed cases containing the nuts ripen and plummet to the ground. Each seed case is a globe-like structure with a fragile, rough, outer shell and a tough, fibrous, inner shell, a quarter inch (6 mm) thick. Inside, between eight and twenty-four Brazil nuts are arranged like sections of an orange. A seed case, approximately six inches (15 cm) in diameter, weighs between three and four pounds (1.5 and 2 kg). From 100 to 150 feet (33 to 50 m), a falling seed could cause instant death to man or beast below.

The *castanheiros,* or gatherers, stay clear of the trees in windy weather and confine gathering to midday, when there is the least likelihood of danger. Still, their job is a perilous one. The Amazon River is the highway of the Brazil nut trade, and *castanheiros* depend upon ample rainfall to permit navigation of the rivers that penetrate the jungle. In winter, the gatherers travel inland, setting up crude shelters near the Brazil nut groves. For the duration of the harvest, they will live off the land.

With machete-type knives, the gatherers remove the seed cases to reveal the three-sided nuts, place them in rattan baskets, and then dip them into streams for cleaning. The nuts are dried in primitive shelters, and are transported by mule or canoe to the local *barracao* or gathering place. Here the *castanheiros* are paid in cash or merchandise for their efforts.

The nuts are thoroughly dried in automatic, rotating dryers, and the best are selected manually and packed for export in 110-pound (50-kg) bags. Those to be shelled are soaked in water for 2 hours, then boiled 5 minutes to soften the shells, which are cracked by hand. Good kernels are dried and graded for quality and size, then sealed in vacuum-packed bags.

More Brazil nuts are exported in the shell than shelled (approximately 60,000 tons per year). The United States is the largest importer, followed by the United Kingdom, West Germany, Italy, France, Australia and the Netherlands.

The United States was one of the last countries to enjoy Brazil nuts. In 1569, the Cayanpuxes Indians of Peru introduced the Brazil nut to Spanish commander Juan Alvarez Maldonado, who fed them to his hungry troops. Dutch traders were shipping Brazil nuts to the Netherlands by 1633, but it wasn't until the 1800s that Yankee clipper ships carried the Brazil nut, along with rubber, cocoa and cashews to the United States, where the Brazil nut soon became a choice tidbit in the toe of Christmas stockings.

"The fresh Brazil, which Nature has decreed shall not be ready for the English Christmas, is a good nut … when however, it has been kept for a year or so it takes an oily nature which only the most active of livers can painlessly discuss. At this stage it should be lighted with a match to amuse the children…"

EDWARD A. BUNYARD,
THE ANATOMY OF DESSERT, 1933

Because of their delicate taste, Brazil nuts are often substituted for almonds in recipes.

Brazil Tree

- **SIZE:** *100–150 feet (33–50 m)*
- **AVERAGE LIFE SPAN:** *More than 100 years.*
- **BEARS:** *8th year*
- **MATURE YIELD:** *At 12 years, 250–500 pounds (115–230 kg) in alternate years.*
- **CLIMATE:** *Tropical*
- **HARVEST SEASON:** *January to June*

- **COMMERCIAL AVAILABILITY:** *Unshelled, shelled, skins on, blanched, whole, chopped.*
- **SELECT:** *Unshelled Brazil nuts free of cracks or openings in the shell. Fresh shelled nuts should have a tender texture due to a high oil content.*
- **STORE:** *In tightly sealed containers, kept in the dark at a temperature of less than 70° F (21° C).*
- **TO SHELL:** *Place nuts in a saucepan and cover with water. Add salt (1 Tbsp per quart of water/15 ml per 1.2 L). Boil gently for 3 minutes. Drain, cool and crack quickly with a nut cracker.*

TO ROAST (UNSHELLED): *Place nuts in shell on a baking sheet and bake 20 minutes at 400° F (200° C). Open with a nut cracker. Nuts will have a toasted flavor and come out of the shell easily.*

TO BLANCH (SHELLED): *Place nuts in saucepan and cover with water (1 quart for each pound of nuts/1.2 L for each half kilogram). Add 1½ tsp (7 ml) baking soda to help dislodge the skins. Simmer 2 minutes. Remove skins while warm.*

TO SLICE: *Place the nuts in a saucepan and cover with cold water. Bring to a boil and simmer 2 minutes. Drain and slice.*

NUTRITIONAL VALUE: *Brazil nuts are the best natural source of the amino acid methionine. They are rich in calcium, iron, vitamin A and unsaturated fat (30 percent linoleic acid) and are high in enzymes.*

Cashew

Genus: Anacardium occidentale

Family: Anacardiacae

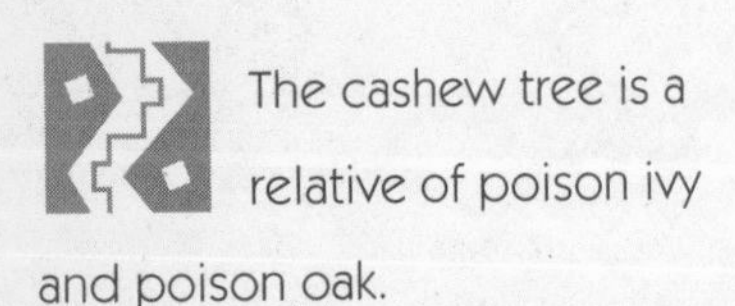

The cashew tree is a relative of poison ivy and poison oak.

"When was the last time you shelled a cashew? The answer is never. That's because these rich, butter-flavored nuts are potentially lethal in the shell.

The cashew tree, a hardy, fast-growing evergreen, can range from a small shrub to a 40-foot (13 m) tree, with a symetrically shaped, umbrella-like canopy. It is the only tree known to bear fruit with an exterior seed.

Before the nut develops, the tree blossoms for two to three months, and the flowers grow in clusters at the end of the branches. When flowering stops, seedcases sprout at the branch tips. The seed-case is olive-green, and kidney-shaped, like the nut inside. When ripe, the seed case will turn red and fall off the tree. The stalk or, peduncle, which supports the flower, swells between the nut and the stem, producing the cashew apple. This juicy, thin-skinned fruit is actually pear-shaped and may be yellow or red. It is eaten locally and made into jams, jellies, wine, vinegar and juice.

The cashew, which can grow up to 1½ inches (4 cm) in size, is encased in two shells. The outer shell is smooth, thin and somewhat leathery. The inner shell is considerably tougher and must be cracked to be removed. Between the two layers is a honeycomb membrane containing a toxic, brown oil, which can cause extreme blistering of the skin. The caustic resin is removed by heating the cashew seed-case to a temperature where the outer shell explodes, releasing the toxins. The oil is used in lubricants, in pesticides, and in the production of plastics.

Following roasting, the nuts are shelled, either by hand with a mallet, as done in India, or by a mechanized process like those used in Africa. The nuts are then dried and the skins removed by rubbing. The cashews are graded according to size and color and packaged for export in 25-pound (11-kg) tins.

The cashew entrepreneur is always faced with a dilemma — whether to harvest the apples, which will be past their prime when the nuts are ready to be picked, or the cashews. When the cashews are harvested, the apples are left to rot. They ferment within 24 hours of losing the nut and become too astringent for use.

The cashew is believed to have originated in north eastern Brazil, near the equator and parts of the West Indies. In the eighteenth century Brazilian natives called the nut *acaju.* Spanish sailors introduced the cashew to Panama and Central America in the sixteenth century. Portuguese colonists and missionaries took the nuts to east Africa and Portuguese India (Goa). The Portuguese knew the nut as *caju,* from which the English word cashew derived.

Cashews have been called the poor man's crop but the rich man's food, because 97 percent of the world's cashews come from wild growth and small farm holdings. Cashews rank among the most expensive nuts because of the labor involved in cracking the shell. India is the world leader in cashew production, followed by Mozambique, Tanzania, Brazil, Kenya, Madagasgar and Thailand. Over 90 percent of the world's cashew products are consumed in North America.

Cashews are best as a cocktail nut, but they also make a wonderful nut butter. They're delicious in salads, casseroles, beef stew, stuff-

Sixteenth-century botanists called the cashew *elephanten lause,* elephant louse, a name depicting its fat, curvy shape.

ings for chicken, and in cakes and cookies. Cashews are used in Oriental and Indian cooking, including vegetable and rice dishes, lamb and curry.

French naturalist A. Thevet provided the first drawing of the cashew in 1558, after visiting Maranhao in northern Brazil.

Cashew Tree

- **SIZE:** *Shrub size to 40–50 feet (13–15 m)*
- **AVERAGE LIFE SPAN:** *30 to 40 years*
- **BEARS:** *3rd to 4th year*
- **MATURE YIELD:** *At 7 years, 20 pounds (9 kg) (unhulled) per tree per year, 6 pounds (3 kg) (shelled) per tree per year.*
- **CLIMATE:** *Easily cultivated in well-drained, low elevations of the tropics.*
- **SPECIAL REQUIREMENTS:** *Annual rainfall of 40 to 120 inches (100–300 cm).*

- **COMMERCIAL AVAILABILITY:** *Whole, pieces, roasted, salted, plain.*
- **SELECT:** *Raw cashews that are white, pale ivory or light ash in color, dry, and free from insect damage.*
- **STORE:** *Refrigerated in airtight containers.*
- **TO ROAST:** *Spread cashews in one layer on baking sheet; bake until brown at 300° F (150° C), stirring often.*
- **NUTRITIONAL VALUE:** *Cashews are a good source of vitamins D, Bl and iron.*

Chestnut

Chestnuts bring out the romance in nut lovers — visions of these lustrous round nuts roasting over an open fire, of street vendors, and passers-by savoring the sweet, delicate taste of the chestnut. Perhaps the most festive and most fleeting of all the edible nuts, fresh chestnuts are available in time for Thanksgiving and Christmas, but are gone by the end of January.

Until the early 1900s, it was a holiday tradition in the United States to gather wild chestnuts. At that time about 25 percent of the hardwood forests in the area east of the Mississippi River were American chestnuts. This beautiful tree reached heights between 70 and 100 feet (23–33 m) with a diameter up to 4 feet (1 m). It was the most important food and timber species in the hardwood forest.

The chestnut tree is not to be planted on an average size lot, even though severe pruning can restrict growth by half. Since chestnut trees are menoecious, having male and female flowers on the same tree, cross-pollination is necessary, thereby requiring trees to be planted in pairs, within 200 feet (66 m) of each other.

Size is not the only reason for planting chestnuts well away from the house. Many find the odor of their pollen offensive. Also, the trees shed ample amounts of catkins in summer and spiny burrs in autumn, in addition to their leaves. Yet, thoughts of chestnuts roasting on the fire make it all worthwhile.

The chestnut produces three nuts in a "cup," which is protected by spiny bars. Improved cultivated varieties contain a single large nut.

GENUS: Castanea

FAMILY: Fagaceae

"When chestnuts were ripe I laid up half a bushel for winter. It was very exciting at that season to roam the then boundless chestnut woods of Lincoln . . ."

WALDEN, OR LIFE IN THE WOODS

HENRY DAVID THOREAU, 1854

There is fossil evidence that chestnuts existed during the middle Tertiary period, approximately 65 million years ago.

Under a spreading chestnut tree
The village smithy stands.

THE VILLAGE BLACKSMITH
HENRY WADSWORTH LONGFELLOW, 1839

The sweet-tasting kernel is protected by a bitter skin and an outer shell that must be removed before eating.

Nuts are ripe when burrs split to release 1 to 3 nuts. Gather the nuts immediately to avoid deterioration and wildlife. Rake chestnuts into piles and gather into polyethelene bags or ventilated cans to allow moisture to escape.

Chestnuts were both a staple food source for peasants and popular treat sought after by nobility. Made famous by the French, *marrons glacés* is a special chestnut confection that takes twelve steps to create. The Dupon Nemours family, who emigrated from France before the Revolution of 1789, is credited with introducing the European species of chestnut to America. Thomas Jefferson also played a role in its propagation, grafting branches onto American root stock in the Virginia area.

Unfortunately, in 1904 the chestnut blight fungus, *Endothia parasitica*, was identified in the New York City Zoological Park, and was believed to have come from northeast Asia on imported Asiatic trees. The fungus spores of the deadly disease, carried by birds, insects and wind, spread the fungus between Maine and Georgia, and within approximately forty years, the entire natural range of the American chestnut — an estimated 9 million acres (4 million hectares) of this stately tree — was eliminated, along with the tradition of gathering nuts.

Longfellow's legendary chestnut tree, felled amidst a great deal of protest in 1876, has since proved to have been a horse chestnut tree, when a chair made from the timber was examined under the microscope.

The chestnuts we enjoy today are either imported from Italy or come from other species now grown in the United States. Fortunately for North American consumers, developments are being made in local chestnut propagation. In the Pacific Northwest, botanist and forestry consultant Omroa Bhagwandin is studying chestnut cultivation, and experimenting with European and Asian chestnut varieties near Morton, Washington. Since 1983, horticulturalists at Chestnut

Hill Nursery in Alucha, Florida have been producing blight resistant nursery stock, the first to receive a U.S. Plant Patent. There are also a number of small growers in the U.S. who market smaller, shrub-like Asian chestnuts. The Spanish chestnut (*Castanea sativa*) also known as the European or Italian, grows only west of the Rockies. The Chinese chestnut (*Castanea mollissima*), popular because of its immunity to fungus, is hardy enough to grow in the east, where there is commercial production in Maryland and Georgia.

Horse chestnut trees are botanically unrelated to true chestnuts. Their fruits are unpalatable and are fed only to cattle and sheep. Edible varieties of chestnuts are relatives of the beech and oak families.

In pre-Columbian times, North American Indians ate chestnuts and ground them to make a doughy bread. In southern Europe and some of the mountainous areas chestnuts were essential to life, eaten raw, roasted, stewed, dried and ground into flour. This sweet-flavored flour was used to make porridge, polenta, yeast-cake, and fritters. Even today, chestnuts are a basic food in Sardinia, Corsica, the Massif Central and parts of northern Italy.

It is the French who have brought the status of the chestnut to luxury food in the form of purées, creams and *marrons glacés,* a special convection that takes twelve steps to make. The French even distinguish between chestnuts grown for this purpose, called *marrons*, and those growing wild or cultivated for ordinary use, known as *châtaignes*.

Marrons are a specialty of the Ardèche region of France. The biggest and best marrons are grown in Lyon, where they are candied into *marrons glacés* in Privas.

Since 1882, chestnut cream, made from a purée of sweet chestnuts, fragments of *marrons glacés*, sugar and glucose has been manufactured in Ardèche. The cream is used in confectionery and pâtisserie industries.

Will the blight end the chestnut?
The farmers rather guess not.
It keeps smoldering at the roots
and sending up new shoots
Till another parasite
Shall come to end the blight.

EVIL TENDENCIES CANCEL
ROBERT FROST, 1930

In ancient times, chestnuts were the source of many medicinal remedies. The leaves were utilized in tinctures to treat chilblains, eczema, rheumatic and neuralgic pains, while the bark was taken internally to treat ulcers and fever, and chestnut powder was said to relieve colic and intestinal disorders.

English diarist John Evelyn (1620–1706) believed the chestnut was underrated as a food in England because of its use as fodder for pigs, and due to its popularity with the poor. "But we give that fruit to our Swine in England, which is amongst the delicacies of Princes in other countries; and being of the larger Nut, is a lusty, and masculine food for Rustics at all times. The best Tables in France and Italy make them a service, eating them with Salt, in Wine, being first rosted on the Chapplet; and doubtless we might propagate their use, amongst our common people, at lest being a Food so cheap, and so lasting."

What's most unusual about the chestnut is that it's more akin to a starchy vegetable than a nut. Freshly harvested kernels contain mostly starch and almost no sugar. As moisture is lost the sugar content increases, producing the distinctive, sweet taste.

Cure chestnuts by spreading in a single layer in a warm area not exceeding 85° F (27° C). Let nuts dry for several days, until they taste sweet. Eating quality greatly improves as starch converts to sugar. As moisture is lost, their tree weight decreases 10 to 20 percent.

Chestnuts are best stored in temperatures between 32° and 36° F (0°–1°C) at 85 percent relative humidity. Chestnuts will store throughout the winter in a fruit cellar if packed in clean, slightly damp sand, sawdust or peat moss.

Chestnuts may be roasted in their shells and simply peeled and eaten. Peeled chestnuts may also be puréed, with or without sugar, preserved or frozen, grilled, boiled, or cooked in butter, milk or broth. They can be served as a vegetable on their own, or as a perfect accompaniment with fowl and game. After cooking, chestnuts resemble potatoes in texture, and are not suitable in recipes requiring crisp nuts.

Chestnut flour is made by grinding dried chestnuts. Gluten free, it adds a distinct flavor to cakes, breads, pastas and puddings, and can be utilized in making sauces, and thickening soups and gravies.

Chestnut tree

VARIETIES: *Japanese (ornamental only); Spanish (west of Rockies); Chinese (east of Rockies). Abundance, Crane, Kuling, Meiling, Orrin.*

- **SIZE:** *60–100 feet (20–33 m); 40-foot (13 m) tree spread.*
- **AVERAGE LIFE SPAN:** *50 years*
- **BEARS:** *3rd to 5th year*
- **MATURE YIELD:** *40–70 pounds (18–32 kg) per tree.*
- **CLIMATE:** *USDA zones 5–8; slightly hardier than the peach; winters no cooler than -15° F (-26° C).*
- **WHEN TO PLANT:** *Autumn (west of Rockies); early spring (east of Rockies)*
- **PLANT:** *In well-drained acidic soils, pH 5.5 to 6.5; (intolerant of alkaline soils) in full sun, with fair to good drainage (dampness causes fungus).*
- **SPECIAL REQUIREMENTS:** *One inch (2.5 cm) of water per week.*
- **FERTILZER:** *Spring only (10–10–10 or something similar).*
- **HARVEST SEASON:** *September to November*

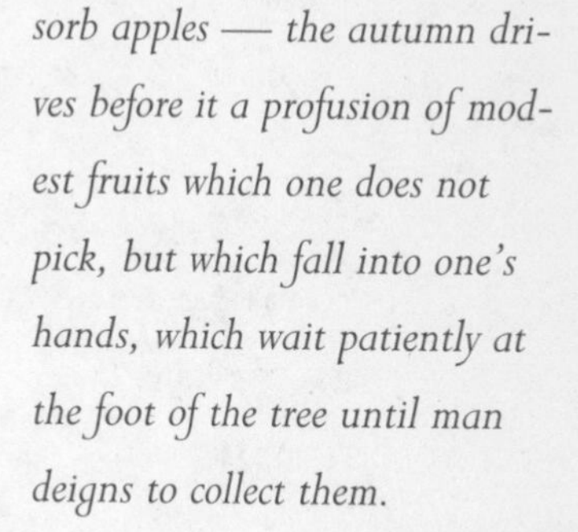

Chestnuts in their spiky cases, squash medlars, and tart-tasting sorb apples — the autumn drives before it a profusion of modest fruits which one does not pick, but which fall into one's hands, which wait patiently at the foot of the tree until man deigns to collect them.

EARTHLY PARADISE
COLETTE, 1966

Keep a chestnut, begged or stolen, in your pocket as a charm against rheumatism.

ANONYMOUS

Greek soldier Xenophon, who lived around 400 B.C., is said to have fed his entire army with chestnuts during one of his campaigns in Asia Minor.

In Europe, the chestnut is eaten as a sweetmeat on St. Simon' s Day and is distributed to the poor on the feast of St. Martin.

COMMERCIAL AVAILABILITY: *Fresh whole; dried and peeled; canned whole and roasted; chestnuts in syrup; chestnut paste; chestnut purée (sweetened or natural); marrons glacés.*

SELECT: *Plump chestnuts with unblemished shells. Properly cured, chestnuts should feel firm when pressed, having a slight air pocket between the nut meat and the shell. Shriveled or blistered skin is indicative of mold. Tiny holes in the shell suggest the presence of worms. Wash chestnuts before preparing and discard any that float.*

STORE: *Dried, peeled chestnuts keep indefinitely in airtight containers. To use, treat like dried beans by soaking overnight.*

TO DRY: *First cut a slash in the shell without piercing the nut meat, to allow hot air to escape. Place chestnuts on a baking sheet in the oven at a low temperature with the oven door ajar.*

TO ROAST: *Place slashed chestnuts on a baking sheet, sprinkle generously with water and bake 15 to 20 minutes at 400° F (200° C). Chestnuts may also be roasted on top of the stove, over a wood stove or open fire. Place slashed nuts in a skillet or popcorn shaker, cook over medium heat for 20 minutes, shaking frequently. Microwave slashed chesnuts on high for 2 minutes.*

Regardless of cooking method, shell and peel chestnuts while still hot. Chestnuts are done when the shell curls away from the cut. Nut meat will be yellow, soft and sweet smelling.

TO PEEL CHESTNUTS FOR COOKING: *Slash shells as explained previously. Place in a baking pan with a little water and roast 8 minutes at 400° F (200° C). Peel while still hot.*

Chestnuts may also be halved, slicing from the pointed end to the bottom. Place in a pot and just cover with water. Boil 5 minutes and remove with a slotted spoon. Shell and peel while still hot.

NUTRITIONAL VALUE: *Chestnuts are the most superior nut nutritionally speaking, being more like a grain than a nut. Chestnuts compare favorably with brown rice but contain almost no sodium. Low in fat and cholesterol free, chestnuts are high in carbohydrates and contain protein in the correct amount for a balanced diet. The protein is of outstanding quality, comparable to that of an egg.*

Chestnuts have the least number of calories (190 per 100 grams) and fat content (2.74 per 100 grams) of all the edible nuts. They are roughly 45 percent carbohydrate in starch form, 5 percent oil, and 50 percent moisture.

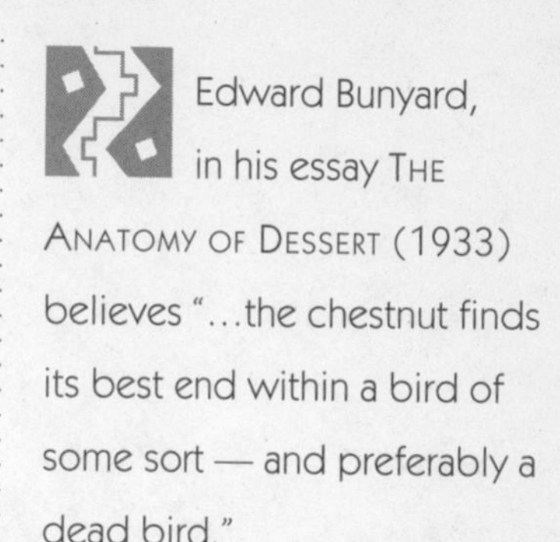

Edward Bunyard, in his essay THE ANATOMY OF DESSERT (1933) believes "...the chestnut finds its best end within a bird of some sort — and preferably a dead bird."

The chestnut is thought to have been named for Castana, a city in Greece where the tree was abundant. *Castana* is also the Spanish word for chestnuts. Castanets, clicked by Spanish dancers, are named for chestnuts because of their similar, round shape.

Coconut

GENUS: Cocos nucifera
FAMILY: Palmaceae

If a man were placed on earth with nothing else but the coconut tree, he could live in happiness and contentment.

ANONYMOUS

I associate the superb, sweet taste of coconut with my favorite brand of chocolate bar, a coconut cream I ate as a child on the way to and from school. The large-sized bar came in two sections, perfect for coming and going. The rich, moist taste made the walk seem shorter, especially in winter, warming me right down to my galoshes. Or was it just the effects of day-dreaming about the swaying palms drawn on the wrapper?

I still daydream about swaying palm trees, and every time I see a real one, I marvel at the look of them: their straight, majestic trunks bending slightly away from each other, toward the sun. Of the more than 3,000 species of palm tree, the coconut is the most widely cultivated. It comes in two basic sizes—tall and dwarf—but only the tall one is planted for commercial use. An estimated 600 million coconuts grow in more than 80 countries around the world. The countries that produce coconuts for export are the Philippines, Indonesia, India, Sri Lanka, Mexico, Malaysia and Papua, New Guinea.

The origins of the coconut palm are still debated by botanists. The "Old World theory" says that the coconut palm is indigenous to the Indo-Pacific: there's fossil evidence of coconuts in New Zealand; 3,000 year-old records of coconuts in India; and a plethora of coconut-specific parasites in Southeast Asia. Marco Polo described coconuts in Sumatra and India in 1280. And it's speculated that coconuts reached East Africa via Arab spice traders, and West Africa and Brazil after 1500, via Portuguese sailors.

The "New World theory" suggests coconuts originated in the Pacific coast of Panama. Early Spanish explorers discovered them growing there, and eventually brought the coconut to America in the 1500s. There is also the theory that coconuts were dispersed by ocean currents. However, palm tree botanists doubt that coconuts would survive washed up on salt water beaches, their young shoots ravaged by sand crabs. British palm authority E.J.H. Corner believes coconuts grow only where mankind has intervened to plant them.

The coconut is the world's largest seed and the largest of all the edible nuts. It grows between 8 and 15 inches (20–40 cm) in length, with a diameter between 6 and 8 inches (15–20 cm) and a weight averaging around 7 or 8 pounds (3 or 3.5 kg). It takes the longest time of all the edible nuts to mature on the tree, roughly a year. At 14 months the nuts fall off the tree, or are picked by agile climbers who scale the palms using a sling or a series of notches cut in the trunk.

Coconuts develop year round, 3 to 6 nuts per flower-bearing branch, a dozen or so branches at a time at any stage of development. The nut consists of several layers: a smooth, tan-colored outer layer; a hard, brown, hairy husk with three indented "eyes" at one end (one eye being the place where the young tree will sprout, the other two where the roots will grow); a thin brown skin; the white coconut meat; and at the center, opaque coconut juice.

Eaten raw or cooked, coconut is a substitute for meat and bread for millions of people who live in the tropics. A single nut contains as much protein as a quarter pound of beefsteak, and the juice contained inside the nut provides a refreshing beverage.

Besides being a staple food for some, and a baking and confectionary ingredient for others, the white coconut meat, called *copra* when dried, is pressed to make coconut oil, used in commercial frying, and as a component in packaged goods like candy, margarines,

He who plants a coconut tree plants food and drink, vessels and clothing, a habitation for himself and a heritage for his children.

ANONYMOUS

detergents, synthetic rubber, brake fluid, plastics, and safety-glass. Coconut oil is one of the finest oils for soap, shampoo and cosmetics, as it's rich in glycerins. *Copra* meal is fed to livestock and used for fertilizer.

The name "coco" comes from the Spanish, meaning monkey face. The three scars on the base of the shell are thought to resemble a monkey.

The coconut palm is considered to be one of the most useful trees in existence. The Sanskrit name *"kalpa uriksha"* means "the tree which provides all the necessities of life." Virtually every part of the coconut and the tree is used. For example, the terminal buds and inner areas of young stems are considered a vegetable delicacy. A fermented liquid, called toddy, is extracted from the flower buds and made into a drink or distilled into a liqueur called *arrack* (this drink is boiled down to a sugar called *jaggery*). Coconut leaves are used in roofing and thatching, to make baskets, fans, brooms, mats and fences. *Coir,* coarse fibres in the husk, are made into ropes, cables, brushes, matting, and stuffing for furniture and bedding. Coconut shells are burned for fuel and made into utensils and the "coconut pearl", a lustrous, hard jewel found occasionally in the cavity of the coconut, is made into jewellery. Coconut juice, consumed as a drink and also processed into vinegar, is rich in minerals, vitamins, and sugar.

During World War II, coconut juice was dripped into the veins of patients whenever sterile glucose was unavailable.

Coconut palms flourish close to the sea, although they require fresh water from rainfall and circulating ground water to survive. Palms grow inland and at altitudes up to 2,000 feet (660 m).

Most of the world's coconuts are produced on small native plantations. The single-seeded nut is easily propagated in its unhusked form. Laid on their sides, in nursery beds close together, the nuts are partially covered with soil. After 4 to 10 months, they sprout and are transplanted to the field, spaced 25 or 30 feet (8–10 m) apart. Oddly enough, the sap rises in the tree, not the bark.

Processing begins right in the field. The thick husk is removed by impaling the nut on an upright, iron spike. The nuts are then split

in two with a hatchet, and the halves set out to dry in the sun for two or three days, or in heated kilns for four or five days.

The meat is removed from the shells and the natural moisture content reduced by approximately 50 percent to 5 or 6 percent. The coconut is then graded into six classes and bagged for export.

In North America coconut is at its best baked in cakes, cookies and desserts in dried form. Coconut meat is used fresh in India, Africa, Indonesia and South America, in condiments and for seasoning raw vegetables and fish, or as an ingredient in chicken, beef and shellfish stews. Coconut milk, made with equal amounts of water and shredded coconut, gives curries, sauces and rice dishes a distinctive, smooth taste in Indian dishes. Polynesians utilize it in soups, jams and marinades. In Vietnam and the Philippines pork, beef and poultry are marinated in a mixture of one part water and four parts shredded coconut. In Brazil and Venezuela coconut cream is poured over desserts and pastries.

Coconut milk and cream are basic ingredients in southern Indian and Southeast Asian cooking, particularly *molee*, or sauces. They are essential elements of Indonesian and Malaysian cuisine, and are used as thickening agents. In West Africa, Colombia and Brazil, coconut adds flavor to rice dishes.

Coconut Tree

- **SIZE:** *60–100 feet (20–22 m)*
- **AVERAGE LIFE SPAN:** *60–80 years*
- **BEARS:** *6th to 7th year*
- **MATURE YIELD:** *At 7 years 75–200 nuts annually.*

The Indian nut alone
Is clothing, meat and trencher,
drink and can,
Boat, cable, sail mast, needle,
all in one.

GEORGE HERBERT
(1593–1633)

Our allowance for the day was a quarter of a pint of coconut milk and the (coconut) meat which did not exceed two ounces for every person.

CAPTAIN WILLIAM BLIGH,
DIARY NOTE, MAY 6, 1789

CLIMATE: *Moist; tropical areas.*

WHEN TO PLANT: *All year round; may be transplanted after 1-4 years.*

SPECIAL REQUIREMENTS: *Water and temperature of at least 72° F (22° C) most of the year.*

COMMERCIAL AVAILABILITY: *Fresh (whole, year-round, especially October through December); sweetened; unsweetened; dried (desiccated); moist; frozen; shredded; flaked; canned (milk, cream, cream of coconut). Don't confuse "cream of coconut," a commercially sweetened product used in desserts and mixed drinks, with "coconut cream" or "milk" made from raw coconut and water.*

STORE: *Unopened coconuts at room temperature for up to six months, depending upon ripeness.*

SELECT: *Coconuts heavy for their size that sound full of liquid when shaken. Reject those with damp eyes.*

PREPARATION: *To drain the liquid from a whole coconut, use an ice pick to pierce the eye that's dark brown and slightly protruding (this eye is easier to pierce than the others). To prepare coconut meat, first drain the liquid. Place the whole coconut in a 400° F (200° C) oven and bake 15 minutes. Remove from heat and break the shell using a hammer. Remove the meat with a knife. To prepare unsweetened coconut milk, combine equal parts of water and shredded fresh or dried unsweetened coconut. Simmer until foamy, then strain through cheesecloth, squeezing out as much liquid as possible. A second, diluted bath may be made from the same coconut. The boiled*

coconut meat should then be discarded. To prepare unsweetened coconut cream, follow the procedure for coconut milk, using one part water to four parts coconut.

REFRIGERATE: *Grated, fresh coconut up to four days; freeze up to six months.*

EQUIVALENTS: *One medium coconut produces approximately three to four cups (.75–1 L), grated.*

NUTRITIONAL VALUE: *Coconuts are rich in calcium, phosophorus, iron, enzymes and carbohydrates. They are a natural source of iodine and vitamin D.*

Hazelnut

GENUS: Corylus
FAMILY: Corylaceae

"O sland'rous world! Kate like
the hazel-twig
Is straight and slender, and as
brown in hue
As hazel-nuts, and sweeter than
the kernels."

PETRUCHIO,
TAMING OF THE SHREW,
ACT II, SCENE I
WILLIAM SHAKESPEARE

The hazelnut, or filbert as it is also known in Europe, probably isn't standard fare in everyone's larder, yet it's the second most plentiful nut in the world. One need only taste French specialities like *gâteau aux noisettes* (hazelnut cake) or *noisettine* (puff pastry with hazelnut butter cream), or *tortone* (Italian nougat), to re-acquaint one's tastebuds with this rich, sweet nut.

Generally nuts that grow wild are referred to as hazelnuts; those cultivated, and usually of European origin, as filberts. The American Joint Committee on Horticulture Nomenclature declared the filbert as the acceptable name for this nut in 1942. However, North Americans still tend to call them hazelnuts.

In Europe, fresh nuts are sold in their husks. The British distinguish between species of hazelnuts, filberts and "cobs" (a familiar hedgerow throughout the English countryside). These distinctions are made according to the relative length of the involucre or husk that surrounds the unshelled nut: filberts have husks longer than the nut; cobnuts have husks and nuts of equal length; and hazelnuts have husks shorter than the nut. Also filberts are longer in shape, cobnuts of medium length, and hazelnuts short and round. However, after the husks are removed, it becomes difficult to distinguish one species from another. The husk or "full beard" as it is called, is one theory of the derivation of the name "filbert". Others purport the nut was named for St. Philibert, whose feast day, August 22, coincides with the European harvest.

There are at least eleven known species of this deciduous tree encircling the globe in northern temperate zones. After the last glacial period in northern Europe, as warmer temperatures developed, the European hazel tree (*C avellana*) spread northward.

Two species were indigenous to North America—*C americana*, located in the east, and *C cornata*, ranging from the Atlantic to the Pacific. Both types are small and produce nuts suitable only for wildlife. Depending upon the variety, the hazel tree can be shrub-like in size or reach heights anywhere up to 120 feet (40 m).

According to old Chinese manuscripts, hazelnuts are as old as agriculture itself, dating back some 5,000 years. Ancient Greeks and romans consumed hazelnuts for medicinal purposes, as well as for food. Cultivation of filberts began in southern Europe, spreading eastward to Turkey. More than two thousand years ago they were exported from the Black Sea. During the 11th century, filberts were traded in the markets of Genoa.

In North America, cultivated varieties were brought from Europe by early settlers who also carried with them all the myths of magic and the occult that surrounded the hazel tree. Hazelnuts were burned on altars as an offering to gods, and branches from the hazel tree were used as divining rods. These rods were used to search for water, hidden treasures and veins of minerals, and even criminals were thought to be discovered by their magic.

Nuts fall to the ground when ripe, with the exception of the "Du Chilly," which must be picked. The hazel-colored shell is thin and brittle, so the nuts must be gathered as they drop to prevent spoiling on the ground.

Nearly 70 percent of the world's growers and exporters of hazelnuts are located in Turkey and northwest Africa. Until the 1940s, the United States imported most hazelnuts. Now they're grown for local

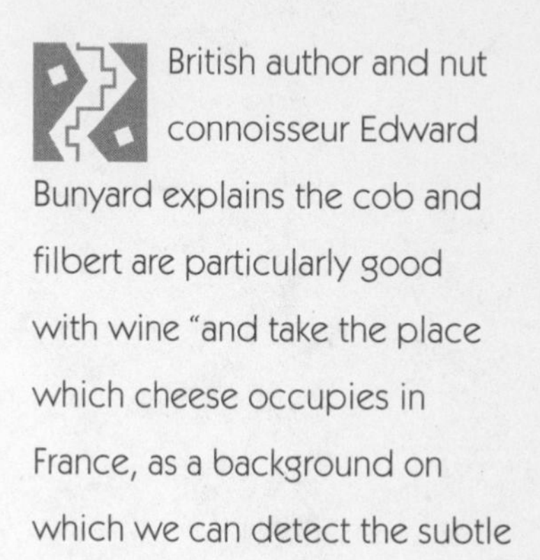

British author and nut connoisseur Edward Bunyard explains the cob and filbert are particularly good with wine "and take the place which cheese occupies in France, as a background on which we can detect the subtle shades of vinous flavor."

Bunyard goes on to say, not only should they be served fresh, in the shell, but with the husks intact, for "...nothing which facilitates the leisurely consumption of nuts is to be discouraged. The quiet selection, removal of the husk and leisurely handling of the crackers are nineteenth-century virtues deserving all encouragement."

THE ANATOMY OF DESSERT, 1933

Filberts put more fat on the body than one would think at all likely.

PLINY

consumption in the Willamette Valley of Oregon, from Hillsboro south to Eugene, and in western Washington state. This represents only about 3 to 4 percent of the total world supply.

In Turkey, hazelnut trees grow in a wild environment, and most of the processing is done by hand. The nuts are picked from the trees, dried in the sun and the husks removed. Shells are broken between revolving millstones, then the nuts are separated from the shells by blowers and the kernels graded according to size.

Eighty percent of filberts are sold shelled. The finest Turkish filberts are round, not pointed, and the best quality come from the Giresun district of the Black Sea.

When processing hazelnuts, there is little waste. Hazelnut oil is extracted from broken nuts. A strong, full-flavored oil, it is combined with lighter oils in salad dressings, sauces, main dishes and baked goods. Rancid or inferior nuts are used for industrial oil, and the shells and husks are burned for fuel.

In the United States, mechanical sweepers pick up the nuts from the ground, separating them from other debris. The nuts are washed and dried to a moisture content of between 8 and 10 percent, and sold shelled or unshelled.

Hazelnuts are eaten raw, roasted, salted; whole, grated or ground. They improve stuffings and terrines, add flavor to savory dishes like chicken and fish, and make wonderful butters. Much of the world's consumption is also based on the confection and pastry businesses.

Spain has created the most extensive cuisine using this nut, culminating in "salsa romesco", a sauce made with filberts and the romesco pepper to accompany shellfish, fish, vegetables and salads.

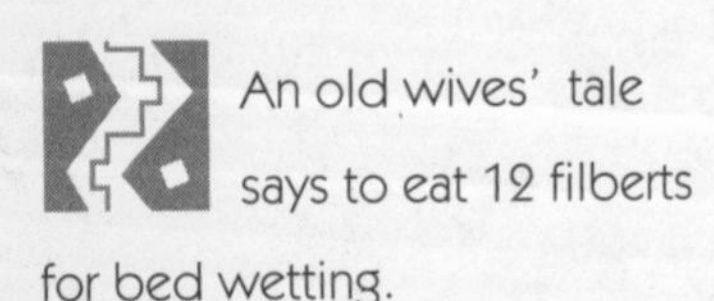

Hazelnut Tree

VARIETIES: *European (Barcelona, Ennis, Du Chilly, Royal); European-American hybrids (Bixby, Buchanan, Potomac, Reed); native American.*

SIZE: *Shrub to 15 feet (5 m) average.*

AVERAGE LIFE SPAN: *50 years*

BEARS: *At 4 years*

MATURE YIELD: *At 7 years, 5–8 lbs (2.5–3.5 kg) per tree per year.*

CLIMATE: *European varieties: USDA zones 6–7 (east of the Rockies), 6–8 (west of the Rockies); European–American hybrids: USDA zone 5; native American: USDA zone 4. Not very frost hardy, yet requires 800 hours per year of temperatures below 45° F (7°C).*

WHEN TO PLANT: *January through March, whenever ground is warm enough to work.*

PLANT: *In deep, well-drained soil in full sun.*

SPECIAL REQUIREMENTS: *Suckers grow constantly and must be trimmed back several times a year before reaching 10 inches (25 cm) in height.*

HARVEST SEASON: *August and September*

October 31st, Hallow's Eve, was also called "nutcrack night". Hazelnuts were cracked, accompanied by fortune telling.

"The hazelnut is a symbol of happy marriages, because its nuts grow united in pairs."

ANONYMOUS

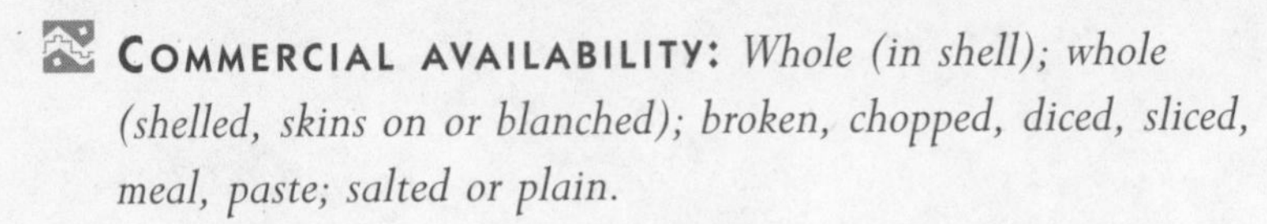

COMMERCIAL AVAILABILITY: *Whole (in shell); whole (shelled, skins on or blanched); broken, chopped, diced, sliced, meal, paste; salted or plain.*

SELECT: *Nuts with shiny shells (not too thick), free from blemishes, holes or cracks.*

STORE: *Refrigerated or frozen in sealed, airtight containers, glass jars or plastic bags, in shell or shelled. The oil content is about 60 percent unsaturated fat, so hazelnuts become rancid at room temperature.*

REFRIGERATE OR FREEZE: *Up to two years. Bring to room temperature before use.*

TO PEEL: *Hazelnuts, like most nuts, are enhanced when lightly toasted. Nuts are easier to chop or grind prior to toasting. To toast, place nuts on a baking sheet and bake 10 to 25 minutes at 350° F (180° C) until lightly browned. Skins can be left on for flavor and texture or removed. Sometimes they are bitter. To remove skins, place toasted nuts, a handful at a time, in a dish towel and rub vigorously.*

NUTRITIONAL VALUE: *Hazelnuts are high in enzymes and vitamin E, a source of sulphur, phosphorus, calcium, potassium, nicotanic acid and vitamins B1 and B6.*

Hickory

You may think you've never tasted a hickory nut, but chances are you have. There are seventeen varieties of hickory trees, all of which bear nuts. Thirteen of these species are indigenous to North America, the most popular being the pecan.

Other edible varieties include the shagbark, mockernut, shellbark, Carolina, and their hybrids. Bitternut and water hickory are inedible because of tannin in the skin covering the kernels. However, the nuts of several hybrids, like the pecan-bitternut and shagbark-bitternut, are edible.

The Algonquian Indians named this family of trees. They also taught colonists in Virginia to use the ripe nuts of the mockernut and shagbark for food. They shelled, boiled and strained the hickories to make a soupy liquid called *pocohicora* or *pohickery*, from which the name is derived. The soup was eaten or cooked slowly with corn meal and made into cakes.

These hardy, deciduous trees are native to the eastern United States and extend westward to Texas and Nebraska. A few species extend into south eastern Canada and northern Mexico. Several types are also found in southeast Asia. Fossil forms indicate that at one time hickories grew over a wider area including the western United States, Alaska, Greenland, Iceland, Europe and considerable parts of China.

Hickories are cultivated to a very limited extent but hybrids, available at nurseries, provide a high quality nut in areas too far north

GENUS: Carya

FAMILY: Juglandaceae

Hickory wood, noted for its hardness, is used for tool handles of hammers, axes, picks and hatchets.

for pecans to grow. Hickory wood, noted for its hardness, is used for tool handles of hammers, axes, picks and hatchets.

Hickory trees are menoecious, having both male and female flowers, and self-pollinate. Four-parted husks encase the nuts, which drop from the husks when ripe. The nuts vary in size and shape from species to species.

Virginian settler Captain John Smith (1580–1631) first recorded the word *pocohicora*, an Algonquian name for a hickory-based soup.

Some hickories have a rich, buttery flavor because of their high oil content—about 70 percent. For that reason, they're generally sold in the shell. Other wild varieties can be quite bitter. Unlike soft-shelled pecans, most hickories have hard shells, which take considerable effort to crack. Soaking nuts in a hot-water bath for 10 to 15 minutes makes shelling easier. Hickory nuts are only available in limited parts of North America, but they are worth keeping an eye out for when enjoying a nature walk.

COMMERCIAL AVAILABILITY: *Whole, unshelled.*

STORE: *In a cool, dry place.*

USE: *As a substitute for pecans.*

NUTRITIONAL VALUE: *Hickories are rich in enzymes. They are a source of iron, magesium, copper and vitamin B1.*

Macadamia

One of the toughest nuts to crack—literally—is the macadamia. It's one of the hardest-shelled nuts in the world, encased in a husk and a nutshell about half an inch (1 cm) thick. For that reason macadamias are sold almost exclusively shelled. But the prize inside is worthy of such protection. The delicate, creamy flavor of the macadamia is a taste treat.

The macadamia is a relatively recent nut, only botanically recognized since 1856. Commercially available for little more than 60 years, it has skyrocketed to international nut status, ranking with the best of them—pine nuts and pistachios—as one of the most tasty and expensive.

The macadamia is indigenous to the subtropical rain forests of southeast Queensland and northern New South Wales, Australia; hence, the names Australian nut, Queensland nut, Australian hazelnut, bush nut or bauple. Until 1856, it was known only to aboriginal tribes of the area. Aborigines called the tree *kindal kindal*. Early settlers liked the tree for shade and its highly ornamental appearance.

Dr. John Macadam, a scientist and philosopher, first drew attention to the nut's edible qualities. In 1856, the Royal Botanical Gardens in Melbourne named the nut after Dr. Macadam.

The first commercial macadamia orchard in Australia was established in 1888 by Charles Staff. This nut became, and remains to this day, the only native Australian crop cultivated commercially.

GENUS: Macadamia
FAMILY: Proteaceae

The macadamia tree is exceptionally attractive. A self-pollinating evergreen, its flowers are creamy white or pink, depending on the species.

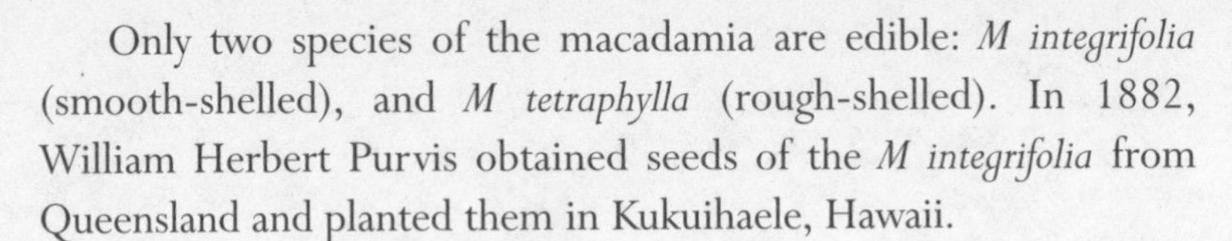

Only two species of the macadamia are edible: *M integrifolia* (smooth-shelled), and *M tetraphylla* (rough-shelled). In 1882, William Herbert Purvis obtained seeds of the *M integrifolia* from Queensland and planted them in Kukuihaele, Hawaii.

However, Ernest van Tassell is considered the father of the flourishing macadamia industry in Hawaii. Half a century after the first trees were planted, it has become a major cash crop.

The nuts first reached Hawaiian stores in 1934 from a total crop yield of 24,000 pounds (10,900 kg). Well over 14 million pounds (6.3 million kg) of shelled nuts are now harvested annually. The cultivation of macadamia nuts is the third largest agricultural industry in Hawaii, after sugar and pineapple.

Hawaii accounts for 90 percent of world macadamia production, entirely of the smooth-shelled variety. The remaining 10 percent are grown in Australia, Africa, Guatamala, Brazil, California and Costa Rica.

Macadamias fall to the ground when ripe, encased in a fleshy, outer husk. Mechanical harvesters pick up the nuts and the husks are removed at the processing plant.

The nuts are dehydrated to a moisture content of 1.5 percent in drying ovens. The shells are then cracked between stainless steel drums.

Unlike most nuts, the flat, rounded macadamia is skinless. (The edible portion of the nut consists of the cotyledons.) The kernels are cleaned, sorted and graded into first, second and inferior categories. They are roasted in refined coconut oil for 15 minutes at 275° F, (140° C), then drained and cooled. Before vacuum packing, they may be lightly salted.

The macadamia is most popular as an appetizer or dessert nut. It is also delicious combined with meat, fish and fruit. To a limited extent, it is used commercially as an ingredient in dairy products, baked goods and candy. In Asia it is added to stews and curries.

Macadamia Tree

- **VARIETIES:** *Smooth-shelled (Beaumont, Keauhou, Ikaika); rough-shelled (Cata, Stephenson).*
- **SIZE:** *Up to 60 feet (20 m); 40-foot (12 m) spread.*
- **AVERAGE LIFE SPAN:** *75-100 years*
- **BEARS:** *5th–7th year*
- **MATURE YIELD:** *At 15 years, 60–150 pounds (20–50 kg) per tree per year (in shell).*
- **CLIMATE:** *USDA zones 8–10 (Florida and especially southern California, but best in Hawaii)*
- **PLANT:** *In deep, rich loam.*
- **SPECIAL REQUIREMENTS:** *Light feedings of nitrogen (California); add phosphorous, zinc and iron (Florida).*
- **HARVEST SEASON:** *When nuts drop; smooth-shell, late Autumn to May; rough-shelled Autumn to February.*

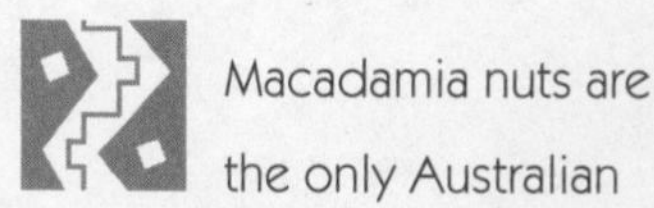

Macadamia nuts are the only Australian food plant to attain international significance.

COMMERCIAL AVAILABILITY: *Shelled: (raw or roasted) whole, halves and pieces; dry roasted diced/large; dry roasted diced (large); (coarse to fine grinds).*

SELECT: *Roasted nuts to ensure freshness.*

STORE: *Vacuum-packed up to two years in a cool, dry place 60°–70° F (16°–22° C).*

REFRIGERATE OR FREEZE: *In sealed containers once opened. Macadamia nuts have a high, unsaturated fat content of 85 percent and easily turn rancid.*

NUTRITIONAL VALUE: *Macadamias are a rich source of folic acid and phosphorus. They contain iron and vitamins A, B1, B2, and B3.*

When is a nut not a nut? When it's a peanut. True nuts grow on trees and peanuts are the seeds of an annual plant that resembles the common garden pea. Botanically speaking, it's a vegetable—a member of the legume family—related to peas and beans.

The peanut is the only plant said to sow its own seeds. Once the bright yellow, self-pollinating flowers bloom on this leafy bush, they swell, then wither, pulling the vines to the ground. The withered blossoms or embryos push down several inches into the soil, where the peanut pods develop with their delicious nuts inside. Peanuts are also called ground nuts, ground peas, earth nuts, goobers, and goober peas.

The peanut is believed to be indigenous to Brazil or Peru, although there are no fossil records. But for approximately 3,500 years, South American pottery vessels were shaped like peanuts with peanut motifs. For centuries, South Americans ground peanuts and mixed them with honey and cocoa. As well, ancient graves of the Incas, found along the Western coast of South America, contained jars of peanuts buried with the dead, thought to provide food for the afterlife.

Before the peanut became the most popular nut in North America, it took a long circuitous route from the New World to the Old World and back again. By the time 16th-century explorers and missionaries came to the New World, peanuts grew as far north as Mexico. Portuguese navigators introduced 2-seeded peanuts from Brazil to both African coasts and the Malabar coast of southwest India.

GENUS: *Arachis hypogaea*

FAMILY: Leguminosae

I hate television,
I hate it as much as peanuts,
But I can't stop eating peanuts.

ORSON WELLES

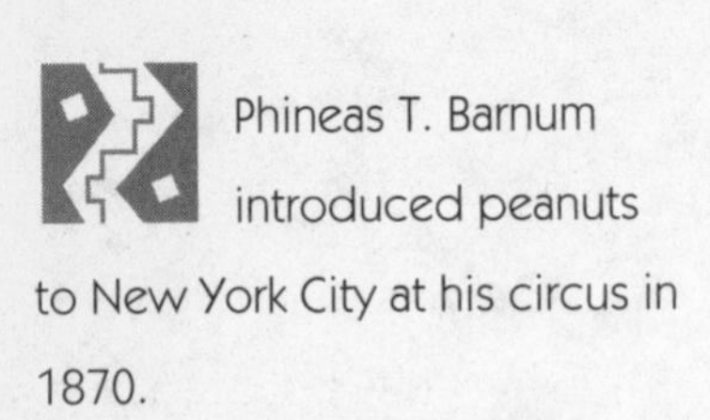

Phineas T. Barnum introduced peanuts to New York City at his circus in 1870.

Spanish explorers took 3-seeded peanuts from Peru to the western pacific, to the Philippines, China, Japan and eastern India.

Portuguese slave traders used peanuts as rations on board ships carrying Africans to America. Once in America, slaves planted peanuts throughout the southern states. Thomas Jefferson (1743-1826) noted that peanuts were grown for home use in Virginia. The first commercial crops for food, oil and a substitute for cocoa, peanuts were raised in South Carolina around 1800.

Peanuts sustained soldiers during the Civil War. At its end in 1865, men of both the North and the South returned home, taking the peanut farther afield and creating a new demand for this new, tasty snack.

Peanuts were roasted by vendors and sold on streets, at ball games and at circuses as a snack food. Phineas T. Barnum introduced peanuts to New York City at his circus in 1870. Peanuts were also eaten in the cheaper seats of theater balconies, which became known as the "peanut galleries." However, peanuts were generally regarded as a food for the poor and fodder for pigs.

Around 1900, the invention of mechanized equipment for planting, cultivating, harvesting, picking, shelling and cleaning peanuts revolutionized peanut farming. In 1920 cotton farmers, ravaged by the boll weevil, converted to peanut farming in Georgia, Alabama and Florida.

After World War I, peanut production increased so rapidly that the government regulated acreage, production and prices in 1935. Controls were lifted during World War II so that increased production could support the war effort, keeping up with the demand for fats and oils. Controls were reinstated again in 1949.

At one time peanuts were only cultivated in tropical and subtropical parts of the world. With superior strains and farming methods, they are now able to grow in areas as far north as Canada, in places where the growing season is at least four months long.

Today, peanuts are one of the world's major food crops, and in America, Congress declared the peanut one of six basic crops. Peanuts are grown in all the southern United States, but the leading producers are Georgia, accounting for 40 percent of the U.S. crop, Alabama, North Carolina, Texas, Virginia, Oklahoma, Florida and South Carolina. Eighty percent of the world's production is grown in Africa and Asia, with India the largest peanut-producing country in the world, followed by China and the United States. Peanuts are a significant food for Third-World countries; India keeps its crop for local consumption. Nigeria is the leading exporter.

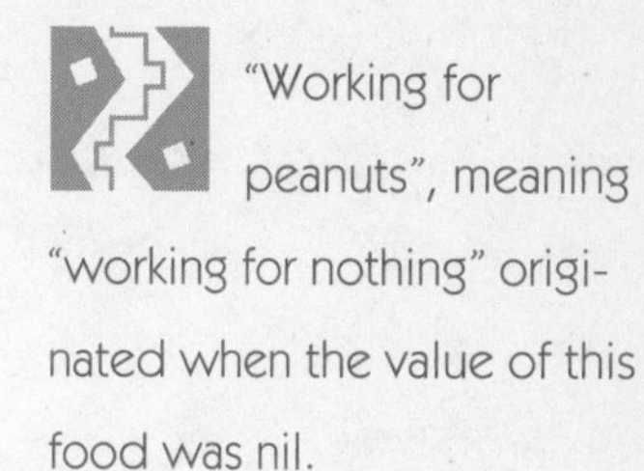

"Working for peanuts", meaning "working for nothing" originated when the value of this food was nil.

Half of the U.S. peanuts are consumed in edible forms, a quarter are exported and a quarter are used for oil, meal, feed and seed. More than half the domestic peanuts are made into peanut butter, and one quarter end up in candy.

Peanuts are the most important oil-bearing seed in the world. Two thirds of the world's peanut crop is crushed for oil. Peanuts, including shells and vines, are one of the most versatile plants on earth. Every part of the plant is used in making more than 300 products, including ink, lipstick, paint, soap, paper, flour, milk, shampoo, cheese and explosives.

To harvest peanuts, lift the entire plant out of the soil. It may require loosening with a fork. If the weather is warm and sunny, peanuts can be left in the sun several hours to dry. Shake off excess

Two Italian immigrants to the US, Amedeo Obici and Mario Peruzzi, founded the Planters Nut and Chocolate Company in Pennsylvania. They held a contest, in 1916, for a company logo. A schoolboy won with a drawing of an animated peanut, which became the famous Mr. Peanut.

soil and hang plants away from access by wildlife in a warm, dry place until pods are brittle. Mature pods have a textured appearance and will open easily; immature pods will still be smooth and should be discarded. Peanuts must be hung in a dry place free of conditions that promote mold. Moldy peanuts should not be eaten as they contain toxins.

The moisture content of the peanut must be reduced from 60 to 70 percent at the time of harvest and to 10 percent for safe, long-term storage. Place unshelled peanuts, one layer deep, on a baking sheet and bake 15 to 20 minutes at 350° F (180° C) (shelled peanuts 15–18 minutes). Remove from oven, cool, shell and salt to taste.

In commercial harvesting, peanuts are mechanically dug from the soil and left in the fields several days to dry. The peanuts are then separated from the vines and dumped into drying wagons to be dried with hot, forced air. The nuts are then taken to buying stations, where they are graded and federally inspected.

Peanuts are one of the nuts we associate with an aroma, as pleasant as the nut itself. In western countries, peanuts are most popular as a cocktail snack and as peanut butter. They're used widely in the candy and confection industry and are extremely versatile in baking and savory dishes.

Indians and Malaysians roast their peanuts and grind them to a paste to make satay, (raw and slightly cooked vegetables served with a spicy peanut sauce), skewered meats and a salad called *gado gado* (sometimes the term refers only to the sauce which is served with rice and vegetable dishes); halved peanuts are ingredients in a savory peanut brittle called *rempeyek kacang*. They also grind their peanuts to make flour. West Africans enjoy a stew-like paste, called *chop*, made with chicken and peanut paste.

Peanut butter is mostly a North American phenomenon. In 1990 we celebrated 100 years of peanut butter, that sticky peanut purée that

coats the roof of your mouth like no other food. It was invented by an anonymous St. Louis doctor in 1890 and fed to invalids because of its nutritive value. People made their own peanut butter until World War I, when industrial manufacturing began. Now there are more than 33 brands available in super markets and approximately 85 percent of all North American households have a jar in their kitchen.

U.S. law requires peanut butter to be 90 percent peanuts—the remaining 10 percent may be salt, sweetners, emulsifiers or hydrogenated vegetable oil.

Peanut butter is made commercially with raw, shelled peanuts that are roasted, cooled and blanched (skins removed). The heart or germ of the kernel, the tiny stem-like protrusion, is removed due to its bitterness. The nuts are then cleaned and ground to an even texture. Emulsifiers may be added as the nutmeats are heated to 170° F (50° C). The mixture is then cooled to 120° F (34° C) to prevent the peanut oil from separating. Coarsely ground peanuts are added to the chunky variety.

High quality peanut butter will retain its flavor and texture for months. Commercial varieties may be stored at room temperature. Unopened, commercial peanut butter will keep in a cool, dry place for one year. Once opened, it will remain fresh for about three months. Beyond three months, the jar should be refrigerated to prevent the oil from becoming rancid. Natural peanut butter will keep for about six months, but it must be refrigerated because it lacks salt, sugar and stabilizers.

Peanut butter is 26 percent protein, which is more than the protein in eggs, dairy products, and many cuts of meat and fish. Although rich in fat (half mono-unsaturated and half poly-unsaturated), peanut butter contains no cholesterol, is low in sugar, starch and carbohydrates. It contains B vitamins, vitamin E, and is rich in iron, calcium and zinc.

The Adult Peanut Butter Lovers' Fan Club is 60,000 members strong. Membership is just $3.00 (U.S.) and includes the club's official newsletter, *Spread the News*.

There's no question that children have a real affinity for peanut butter sandwiches. Between 1971 and 1972, 21,600,000 pounds (9.8 million Kg) of peanut butter were distributed to lunch rooms in the United States by the Department of Agriculture.

Peanut Plant

- **VARIETIES:** *Virginia (2 peanuts per shell, red skin, large kernels used primarily for cocktail and salted nuts); Spanish (2 peanuts per shell, tan skin, small kernel); Runners (2 peanuts per shell, red skin, medium kernel used primarily for peanut butter); Valencia (3 to 4 peanuts per shell, used for roasting and peanut butter.)*
- **SIZE:** *Virginia and Spanish 18 inches (46 cm); Runners (along the ground); Valencia 4 feet (1.3 m).*
- **AVERAGE LIFE SPAN:** *Annual*
- **MATURE YIELD:** *Varies considerably according to variety and length of growing season.*
- **CLIMATE:** *In areas with a minimum of 3,000 corn heat units (4 to 5 months of growing season, depending upon the variety).*
- **WHEN TO PLANT:** *Early to mid-May unless cold, wet weather prevails.*
- **PLANT:** *In light, well-drained sandy to sandy loam soils, free of pebbles; plant in rows 20 inches (0.5 m) apart, 4 to 5 seeds per foot (30 cm), 1½ to 2 inches (3 to 5 cm) deep.*

  Seed houses sell peanuts in the shell that can be planted directly into the ground. However, it is more reliable to shell the peanuts, taking care not to tear the membrane (skin) around the nut.
- **SPECIAL REQUIREMENTS:** *Add lime if pH is below 5.8; irrigate if dry weather persists.*
- **HARVEST SEASON:** *Late September*

COMMERCIAL AVAILABILITY: *Unshelled; shelled; vacuum-packed jars or cans; roasted; dry roasted; salted; blanched; skins on; skins off; chocolate coated; flour; oil; peanut butter.*

SELECT: *Clean, unbroken shells; nuts should not rattle when shaken.*

STORE: *Vacuum-packed, shelled peanuts at room temperature for 1 year. Refrigerate those not vacuum-packed in air-tight containers up to 6 months.*

NUTRITIONAL VALUE: *Peanuts are the top nut for nutritional value; they have the most protein—about 26 percent—and are rich in phosphorus, potassium and magnesium. They contain iron, zinc and calcium and are a good source of vitamins E and the Bs.*

Peanut butter is mostly a North American phenomenon. In 1990 we celebrated 100 years of peanut butter, that sticky peanut purée that coats the roof of your mouth like no other food. It was invented by an anonymous St. Louis doctor in 1890 and fed to invalids because of its nutritive value. People made their own peanut butter until World War I, when industrial manufacturing began. Now there are more than 33 brands available in super markets and approximately 85 percent of all North American households have a jar in their kitchen.

Pecan

Genus: Carya illinoiensis

Family: Juglandaceae

George Washington, a pecan lover, often carried pecans in his pockets. In 1779 he planted seedlings at Mt. Vernon. Thomas Jefferson also planted pecan trees at Monticello in 1779. The trees on both estates still exist today.

Perhaps pecan pie is more American than apple pie. The pecan, best known of the hickory nuts for its buttery-rich, reddish-brown kernel, grows only in the United States. It is the oldest nut tree cultivated in America, thought to be the only tree planted by indigenous people.

Pecans were a dietary staple of Indian tribes, especially those of the Mississippi Valley. Nomadic Indians timed their migration to correspond with the autumn maturing of pecans.

Indians made *powcohicoria*, hickory milk, a rich, nutty paste made by pounding and boiling pecans and straining the liquid. It was also fermented to produce an intoxicating liquor for celebrations at tribal feasts. Spanish explorer de Vada recorded that Indians survived up to two months of the year on pecans alone. Fur traders learned about the pecan from the Indians and helped spread its popularity to the Atlantic seaboard area in 1760. Here it became known as the Illinois nut.

There isn't an accurate record of the first plantings of cultivated pecans; however, it is known that Antoine, a slave gardener on Oak Valley Plantation in Louisiana, had the first success with grafting. By the end of the Civil War he had successfully created 126 trees, the same variety as the famous "Centennial".

By the 1920s the cultivation of pecans spread through 12 states, with Georgia the largest producer, followed by Texas, Alabama, New Mexico and Louisiana.

Native to the temperate climates of Texas, Oklahoma, Arkansas, Louisiana and Mississippi, the pecan is now cultivated widely in the

United States due to irrigation and improved varieties. There are now more than 500 named cultivars. In Texas, where it is the official state tree, there were more than 75 million pecan trees growing wild.

The pecan tree is not to be planted casually in the backyard. The largest tree of their genus, they have been known to reach heights of 180 feet (55 m). They must be planted in pairs for cross-pollination.

The brown, mottled shells of the pecan, cylindrical in shape with a pointed apex, are ripe when the green hull covering the nut splits along suture lines and separates into four sections of equal size.

Initially, pecans were hand harvested when the ripe nuts dropped from the husk. Now, mechanical shakers, nut sweepers, vacuum harvesters, conveyers and trash separators do the task.

Pecans have the highest percentage of fat (72 percent) of any nut, increasing the spoilage factor greatly. Thus, the quality of the pecan is carefully guarded throughout processing. The moisture content of harvested nuts is reduced as quickly as possible to 4.5 percent. The nuts are dried with warm, circulating air at temperatures just under 100° F (35° C), for between 9 and 17 hours. They are immediately refrigerated at 32° F (0° C) and 65 percent humidity to maintain their high quality for a year. If longer storage is required, pecans are frozen. They are shelled only prior to marketing.

Once sized, the nuts are cracked, shelled, graded into 6 categories, dried and packaged. Roughly 85 percent of pecans are sold shelled and more than half of these are sold to the bakery and confectionary industries.

An excellent dessert nut, pecans are probably best in pecan pie or as pralines. Pralines were originally made near Orleans, France during the reign of Louis XV. The original recipe for pralines called for almonds, but during the French Revolution the recipe was taken

The name "pecan" comes from an Indian word that means "a hard shell to crack". The Ojibway word was *pagan*, the Cree and Algonquian, *paccan,* and the Abnuki, *pagann*. The term referred not only to pecans but to the more hard-shelled hickories and walnuts, all members of the same family.

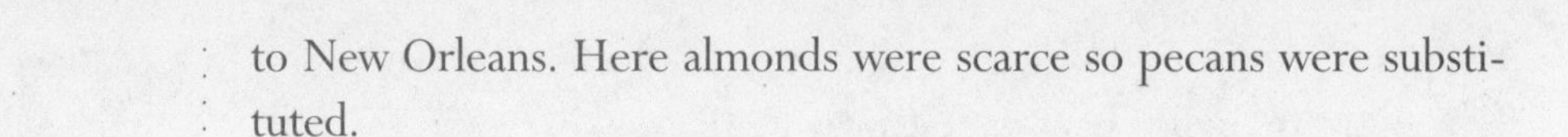

to New Orleans. Here almonds were scarce so pecans were substituted.

Pecans are particularly good in sweet loaves and brownies, as well as savory and vegetarian dishes. They are used commercially in ice cream as well as baking and confectionary industries.

Pecan shells are used as gravel for driveways, as mulch for ornamental plants and fuel for steam boilers. Hardwood from pecan trees is prized for furniture, paneling and flooring.

The world's largest pecan tree is located in Natchez Trace State Park, Henderson County, Tennessee. The tree is 110 feet (37 m) tall with a diameter of 68 inches (172 cm) and a tree spread of 130 feet (43 m).

Pecan Tree

- **VARIETIES:** *Papershells (eastern varieties): Desirable, Choctaw, Cheyenne, Mohawk, Elliott, Sioux; Papershells (western varieties): Western or Western Schley, Wichita; Northern varieties: Fritz, Greenriver, Major, Peruque.*
- **SIZE:** *90 feet (30 m)*
- **AVERAGE LIFE SPAN:** *7 years*
- **BEARS:** *5th–8th year*
- **MATURE YIELD:** *Production increases with age; 25-30 lbs (11–17 kg) at 7 years; 50 to 100 lbs (23–45 kg) at 17 years; up to 800 lbs (363 kg) have been reported.*
- **WHEN TO PLANT:** *Mid autumn to early spring when the ground is neither frozen nor waterlogged.*
- **PLANT:** *In well-drained soil; will not survive in low, boggy ground.*

CLIMATE: *USDA zones 7–10 (Papershells); USDA zones 6–7 (hardy northern varieties); Papershells need 210 days to ripen; hardy northern varieties require 180 days; 60 to 90 inches (2–3 m) annual rainfall.*

SPECIAL REQUIREMENTS: *Zinc applications are needed especially where soil is of a ph of 7.0 or higher.*

HARVESTING SEASON: *Late October to January*

COMMERCIAL AVAILABILITY: *Available year round, peak season in the autumn months; whole (shelled or unshelled); halved; chopped; plain, toasted, salted, spiced.*

SELECT: *Unshelled nuts that are clean, unblemished and without cracks. Kernel should not rattle in shell. Select shelled nuts that are firm, plump, a light, bright yellow color with high oil content that don't appear dried out. To shell, if nuts are dry, soak overnight to increase the percentage of whole kernel. Shell when dry.*

STORE: *Unshelled, tightly wrapped in a cool, dry place for up to 6 months.*

REFRIGERATE: *Shelled nuts up to 3 months in airtight containers.*

FREEZE: *Shelled nuts in moisture-proof containers up to 6 months.*

NUTRITIONAL VALUES: *Pecans are a source of phosphorous, potassium and calcium. They contain iron, copper, magnesium and vitamin C and all the Bs.*

They (pecans) are more delicate in flavor than our own (walnuts), less oily and so fine that the French make pralines of them as good as those made of almonds.

LEPAGE DU PRATZ, 1721

Pine Nut

GENUS: Pinus
FAMILY: Pinaceae

Along with caviar, truffles and saffron, pine nuts are among the most expensive foods we eat, and second most expensive nut on the market after the macadamia. A softer consistency than most nuts, the pine nut is rarely eaten on its own. Rather, its unique, sweet flavor, not unlike almonds but with a more resinous, spicy taste, is added sparingly to a variety of sweet and savory dishes.

The pine nut is actually a seed, found in the cones of some species of pine trees. What makes it so expensive? Jasper Woodruff expresses it best in *Tree Nuts* (1979), saying the trees "grow only under conditions that defy cultivation, fertilization, irrigation, and all kinds of mechanical spraying, harvesting and shelling. All operations are done by hand in competition with rats, birds and insects."

The acquisition of pine nuts is labor-intensive. It takes one ton (900 kg) of pine cones to yield about 75 pounds (35 kg) of seeds. Once the husks are removed, about 25 pounds (11 kg) of pine nuts remain.

There are roughly a dozen species of pine trees that produce edible seeds. They grow in China, Italy, Mexico, South America, north Africa and the southwestern United States. Given their broad range of growth, it's not surprising they're known by a variety of names, including *pignoli, pignoles, pignon, piñolas, pignolia, pinocchi, pinon,* and the Indian nut.

Although pine nuts are now found in gourmet shops and ethnic food stores, they have always been a staple food, second only to

Pine nuts are the largest uncultivated crop in North America, harvested from trees in the wild.

maize, of the Navaho and Pueblo Indians of the southwestern United States. They have more than fifty ways to use pine nuts, including stews, gruels, breads, cakes and pine nut butter.

Carbon dating establishes the pine nut in Nevada some 6,000 years ago. The Indians gathered the seeds of *P edulis*, a low, round-topped, shaggy evergreen, which is still the source of pine nuts in North America today.

P edulis covers millions of acres of arid land in Utah, Colorado, Arizona and New Mexico. These wild stands of trees resemble orchards, often growing with junipers in a distinct plant community known as a pinyon-juniper woodland, at elevations above true desert but below forests of other pines.

This low, shaggy, drought-resistant pine never exceeds heights of 20 feet (6 m). It produces cones wider than they are long, and only bear seeds in the middle 3 to 15 scales. The seeds are ⅜ inch (9 mm) in length, ovoid in shape, and darker in color than the European variety.

P edulis takes roughly 25 years before bearing nuts and doesn't reach full production for 75 years. It has large crops of seeds every three or four years. Processing in the United States is by hand. Collection of the nuts is haphazard and used for local consumption.

The most sought after and most expensive *pignoli* is the *P pinea* or stone pine known as the Mediterranean or Italian pine nut. Native to the Middle East, Provence and Italy, archaeologists found evidence of this pine nut among the household foodstuffs in the ruins of Pompeii.

A statuesque, ornamental evergreen, common to the Riviera landscape, it reaches heights of 80 feet (25 m) with a wide-spreading, umbrella-shaped foliage. It grows in well-established plantations where most of the harvesting is done by hand from October to March.

Many a colonist and native person survived the vigors of inclement weather by robbing the nests of squirrels and rodents for their stash of pine nuts.

The most sought after and most expensive pignoli is the *P pinea* or stone pine known as the Mediterranean or Italian pine nut. Native to the Middle East, Provence and Italy, archaeologists found evidence of this pine nut among the household foodstuffs in the ruins of Pompeii.

Cones are removed from the trees with a hook on the end of a long pole, then dried in the sun. As the scales of the cones open, the seeds are extracted manually by beating the cones. A milling machine separates the seed, which consists primarily of endosperm and several small cotyledons, from its hard husk. Skins are removed before the pine nuts are graded and sized.

The torpedo-shaped kernels of *P pinea* are ⅝ inch (14 mm) in length, thin-shelled and ivory in color. They are exported primarily by Italy. The pignons of Spain and Portugal come from the royal pine tree. The Chinese pine is different again: the nut is beige, tear-drop-shaped and quite pungent, with a more pine-resin flavor, and it's about half the price of the European variety. The seeds of some Chinese species are pressed for oil, used in cooking and for lamp oil.

Pine nuts are probably best known as pesto sauce, an Italian specialty made with pine nuts, fresh puréed basil and cheese. In Sicily, pine nuts are added to pasta dishes. Middle East cookery combines them with rice and currant stuffing in grape leaves, and other *dolmas* (stuffed vegetables and fruits), sweetmeats, pilafs and other stuffings. In China, pine nuts are an ingredient in sweets and used as a garnish in savory, fried dishes. Koreans add them to *congee*, *kimchi* and rice. In Spain and Portugal, they're an ingredient in *paella* and salted cod. Tunisians toss several in iced tea.

Like peanuts, pine nuts can be eaten raw, roasted or salted. They add texture to salads, spinach, eggplant and roasted pepper dishes and may also be ground and used as a coating for fish.

COMMERCIAL AVAILABILITY: *Raw, roasted, salted, chocolate coated, in pesto sauce.*

SELECT: *Ivory-colored nuts, consistent in color without light or dark blemishes.*

STORE: *In airtight containers.*

REFRIGERATE: *Up to 3 months.*

FREEZE: *Up to 9 months (although they tend to become mushy).*

TOAST: *To release full flavor, layer on a baking sheet at 350° F (180° C) for 5 minutes. Watch carefully as they can burn.*

NUTRITIONAL VALUE: *Pine nuts are rich in phosphorus and contain calcium, iron, enzymes and vitamins A, B1, B2 and B3.*

Pistachio

GENUS: Pistacia vera
FAMILY: Anacardiaceae

The Queen of Sheba indulged her passion of the nut by monopolizing the entire pistachio production of Assyria.

Pistachios were called "nuts of paradise" by the Mogul emperors.

This nut made pistachio ice cream what it is today. It is prized for its ornamental, pale-green kernel unique among nuts because it is green (not just on the surface, but all the way through; the greener the more expensive), and its delicate, subtle flavor.

The pistachio is the pit of a red-hulled fruit that grows in clusters, like grapes. It has a reddish skin, enclosed in a pale tan shell that's surrounded by a brownish husk. The pistachio has incited men to jealous rage, battling over forest rights where it grew wild, engaging in bloody feuds that lasted decades. The pistachio was to the nomads of Asia and the Middle East what the pine nut has been to the American Indian—a significant source of nourishment when other food was scarce.

Carbon dating of a nut found in 1965 at Beidha in Jordan establishes its date as 6,760 B.C. This is the earliest, authentic historical record of an edible nut.

A deciduous tree and distant relative of the turpentine tree, the pistachio is thought to have been indigenous to Asia Minor. The tree grew wild, from neolithic times to the 1900s, spreading east as far as Afghanistan and west to countries surrounding the Mediterranean. The nut was introduced to Rome by Vitellius, during the reign of Tiberius. Today, it is widely cultivated in warm and temperate climates, including California.

Turkey, Italy and Syria are among the top world producers, but it is Iran that is the world's pistachio leader, with production centered in the Kerman region.

Iranian pistachios were first introduced to the United States in 1854. In New York, immigrants from the Middle East readily consumed them. During the 1920s and 30s, red pistachios, dyed because of mottling on the shells from the slow method of hand processing, were available to the general public through vending machines. Dying the nuts was not a Middle Eastern custom. It is said to have originated with a Brooklyn street vendor named Zaloom who wanted to distinguish his pistachios from the competition.

William E. Whitehouse, an American plant specialist, spent six months in Iran, seeking the best pistachios. In 1929 he returned to the United States with a 20-pound (9-kg) sack of seeds and established the first plantings in the desert climate of the San Joaquin Valley. The first commercial crop of 1.5 million pounds (700,000 kg), grown on less than 1,500 acres (600 hectares) was finally available in 1976. A number of unrelated events dramatically change the world's pistachio production, making California the world's second largest producer of pistachio nuts.

The fall of the Shah of Iran, construction of an aquaduct in California, and an American tax incentive helped undermine the sale of Iran's pistachios to America and increase production in California by one hundred fold. The California Pistachio Association formed in Fresno in 1972, but it wasn't until 1979 that pistachio production became economically significant. When the Internal Revenue Service allowed Americans to invest in tax-sheltered pistachio orchards, "seed money" financed significant advances in growing techniques and mechanized harvesting. The result: a larger pistachio [as few as

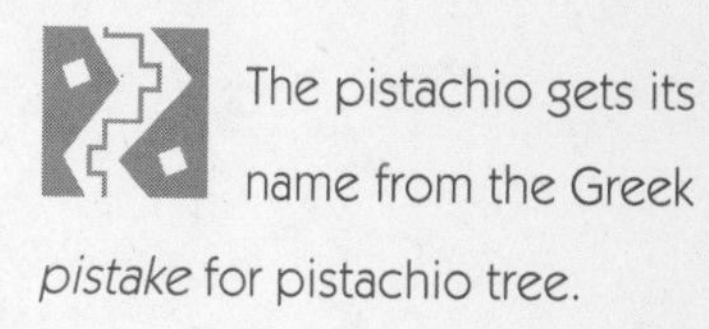

The pistachio gets its name from the Greek *pistake* for pistachio tree.

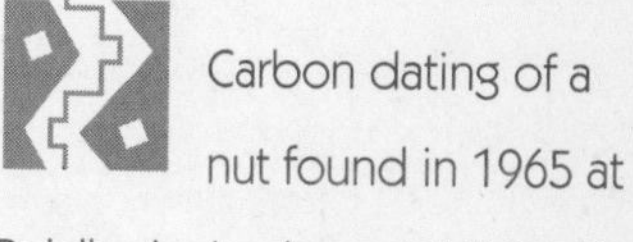

Carbon dating of a nut found in 1965 at Beidha in Jordan establishes its date as 6,760 B.C. This is the earliest, authentic historical record of an edible nut.

14 to the ounce (30 g)], than the Iranian ones [18 to 40 to the ounce (30 g)], and a better-looking nut, since quick harvesting reduced mottling of the shells.

Controversy still exists as to the merits of homegrown varieties versus the imports. Importers claim pistachios from Iran and Turkey are smaller but tastier, describing those from California as beautiful but tasteless. California producers say they all taste the same but theirs are prettier and easier to open. But some connoisseurs of pistachios will tell you the best are those tiny pistachios grown in Sicily, and rarely exported.

Pistachio trees grow in desert or mountainous areas where the soil is often poor and stony. A member of the peach family, *Anacardiaceae*, they grow best where summers are long and dry and winters are short and cold.

The tree, shaped somewhat like an apple tree, is dioecious, having male and female flowers on different trees. Usually one male tree is required for five to ten female trees for proper pollination. Those not properly fertilized will bear nuts that are hollow. The pistachio is a biennial bearer (alternating heavy and light yields).

The tan-colored shell splits in half, along suture lines, exposing the nut when it's ripe. It is said to smile. In Iran the term is *khandan*, laughing. If the weather is unfavorable, the shells won't split.

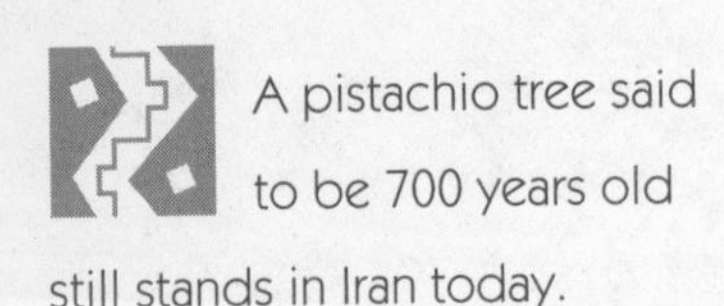

A pistachio tree said to be 700 years old still stands in Iran today.

Harvesting is fully mechanized in California, but manual in other countries where the labor force is primarily female. Women hand pick the nuts or knock them off the tree with poles and dry them in the sun. The drying process is slow, causing the shells to appear mottled. Nuts to be hulled are soaked in water for easy shell removal, hulled by hand and dried again in the sun.

Pistachios are the only nut to be processed without removing the shells. Approximately 90 percent of the California crop reaches consumers roasted and salted in their shells. The shells are naturally light tan in color. However, many continue to be dyed red, for two reasons, according to the California Pistachio Commission: because many people find that form familiar, and they're easier to identify in a bowl of mixed nuts.

Pistachios are used in North America as a cocktail or dessert nut, in pistachio ice cream, and for ornamentation because of their color. Mediterranean and oriental cooks add them to poultry sauces, stuffings and chopped meat dishes. In India, pistachio purée is used to season vegetable and rice dishes. Pistachios complement pork, poultry and veal and are used in desserts and confectionery, especially nougat.

Pistachio Tree

- **VARIETIES:** *Kerman (female); Peters (male)*
- **SIZE:** *25–30 feet (8–10 m)*
- **AVERAGE LIFE SPAN:** *30 years*
- **BEARS:** *At 5–8 years*
- **MATURE YIELD:** *At 10 years, 1–2 bushels*
- **CLIMATE:** *USDA zones 7–10, where summers are hot and dry.*
- **WHEN TO PLANT:** *Spring*
- **SPECIAL REQUIREMENTS:** *Soil that drains well; spring feeding of 10-10-10 fertilizer.*
- **HARVEST:** *August and September*

"The pistachio is a symbol of happiness and plenty for lovers who meet in the moonlight beneath its branches."

ANONYMOUS

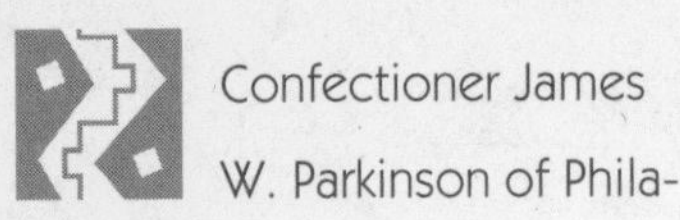

Confectioner James W. Parkinson of Philadelphia, PA, was the first to flavor ice cream with pistachios in 1840.

COMMERCIAL AVAILABILITY: *Year round; shelled (whole or pieces); unshelled (natural; red); raw; roasted; salted; unsalted.*

SELECT: *Nuts with shells partially open, which means they are ripe and easier to shell (pry open using half of another nut shell); closed shells mean an immature nut. Choose shelled nuts that are greenest. To preserve green color, shell, boil in water 2 minutes, drain and remove skins.*

STORE: *In tightly closed containers and refrigerate up to 2 months.*

NUTRITIONAL VALUE: *Pistachios are rich in calcium, thiamin, phosphorous, potassium, iron and vitamin A. They also contains vitamins B1 and B3.*

Walnut

Of all the edible nuts, the most popular one for cooking is the walnut. Its two identical lobes come in more than 100 special cuts and combinations to the delight of cooks. Walnuts are readily available, moderately priced, and retain their flavor when cooked. They're one of the most versatile nuts, lending their familiar crunch to sweet and savory dishes alike.

Seventeen species of walnuts are recognized—all edible. They grow in so many temperate areas of the world and have been growing for so many centuries that the time and place of their origin is difficult to determine.

It is known that walnuts have been collected since prehistoric times for food. Walnut shells have been found in the Swiss Lake dwellings of neolithic man, roughly 7,000 B.C., and walnuts found in Europe date back to the Iron Age.

Of all the walnut varieties, the Persian (also known as the English, Italian and European) is considered the most delicious and the most significant food crop. Thought to have been indigenous to south eastern Europe and temperate Asia, it first spread to Greece and Rome. Walnuts grew around the ruins of the temple of Baalbek and over the walls of Constantinople.

In Greece, the walnut was called *caryon* from the word *kara* meaning head. The Greeks were taken with the resemblance of the shell and kernel to the human skull and brain, and they believed walnuts were a remedy for headaches.

GENUS: Juglans

FAMILY: Juglandaceae

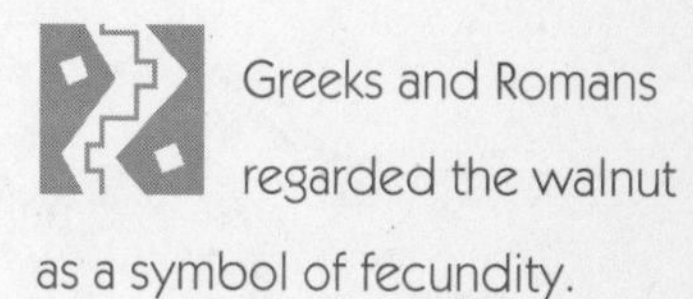
Greeks and Romans regarded the walnut as a symbol of fecundity.

Why, 'tis a cockle or a Walnut-
shell,
A knack, a toy, a trick, a
baby's cap.

PETRUCHIO

TAMING OF THE SHREW
ACT IV, SCENE 3
WILLIAM SHAKESPEARE

In Roman times walnuts were called the Royal Nut and the Nut of Jupiter. Romans, too, believed walnuts had magical and medicinal properties. Roman scholar Pliny wrote "chewing a nut fasting is a sovereign remedy against the bite of a mad dog, if one applies it." Walnuts were thought to be good for decayed teeth, and to relax the belly, especially when consumed with figs.

The Romans extended cultivation of the walnut to France. In the 4th century it was grown in the region of Corésivaudan. It didn't reach England until the 16th century. However it was the English who named them walnuts; "wal" meant "foreign".

In southern Europe, particularly France, walnut oil was used for cooking in place of olive oil. Walnuts made a thickening agent for sweet and savory dishes, and were thought to be a superior dessert nut because they required neither salting nor roasting.

Walnuts were blanched, pulverized and soaked to produce walnut milk, which was a milk substitute in Europe until the 18th century.

English settlers brought the Persian walnut to New England. They called it the English walnut to distinguish it from those they found indigenous to the area, which they named the black walnut for its dark limbs and trunk. Franciscan monks planted the Persian walnut in California while establishing their Spanish missions in the 18th century.

Joseph Sexton started the first commercial orchards at Galeta, near Santa Barbara. He purchased English walnuts, which actually came from South America. By 1869 he had transplanted 200 trees to form an orchard.

Today, California produces almost 100 percent of the United States' walnuts and roughly 90 percent of the world's supply. Other producers include Turkey, China, the former Soviet Union, Greece, Italy, France and Romania.

The black walnut tree, native to the eastern United States and Canada, is the largest of the North American species and the most widely grown nut tree in the United States. Its dark nuts are smaller in size, more circular in shape and stronger in flavor than the Persian variety. Black walnut trees take a long time to bear fruit; demand often exceeds supply. This species is grown more for its hardwood. However, those who appreciate the aggressive flavor of the black walnut can purchase them by mail order.

The walnut is a large, straight, heavy tree, and dark in color. It is not meant for small gardens. Although it is menoecious, having both male and female flowers, its yields are best when two trees are planted together.

The hull of the small green fruit turns brown and usually splits, letting the nut fall to the ground when ripe. Mechanical and hand shaking speeds the harvest. Machines collect, hull and wash the walnuts. They are dried by mechanical dehydrators to a moisture content of 38 percent.

Most walnuts are sold in the shell for export and are shelled for the domestic market. Those in the shell are fumigated and the shells bleached in a dilute sodium hypocloride solution. They are rinsed and rubbed to a uniform tan color, then separated into four sizes for sale. Nuts that are shelled are graded and separated into six sizes.

Walnuts are best served as a dessert nut, "green" (half-ripe) preserved in syrup, and in baked goods like cakes, cookies and pastries. They are excellent in salads, with meat, poultry and fish, and for flavoring sauces, forcemeats (*pâtés* or *rissoles*), and butters.

Green, immature walnuts, including the husks, are edible. In England, a traditional delicacy is pickled walnuts, made from green nuts soaked in salt and water for ten days and placed in vinegar. Green walnuts are also made into marmalades and jams.

Shelled walnuts are sold in France from mid-September until All Saints' day, November first. The French believe walnuts should be eaten within a fortnight of being harvested.

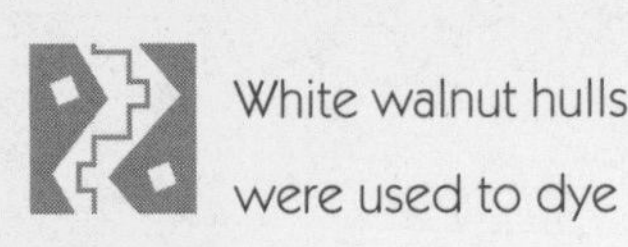

White walnut hulls were used to dye the uniforms of the American Confederates.

Walnut oil, mainly exported from France, should be reserved for salads because of its strong taste and low smoking point. Ratafias and liqueurs are made from walnut husks, and there are walnut-flavored wines. Nut brandy is made from green walnuts. Also, walnut trees, like maple trees, can be tapped for sap in the spring.

Walnut Tree

- **VARIETIES:** *Persian or English which subdivide into the English and Carpathian; Black.*
- **SIZE – PERSIAN:** *60 feet (20 m)*
  BLACK: *100 feet (30 m) (west of Rockies) 150 feet (35 m) (east of Rockies).*
- **AVERAGE LIFE SPAN:** *100 years*
- **BEARS:** *5–10 years*
- **MATURE YIELD:** *At 20 years; alternate years 1–2 bushels, up to 15.*
- **CLIMATE:** *Generally in USDA zones 3–9 with careful selection of varieties outside 6–8; Black: USDA zones 6, 7, 8 (east of Rockies); Black: (west of the Rockies); Carpathians: USDA zones 3–9. English varieties must be matched with local climate.*
- **WHEN TO PLANT:** *Spring or autumn (where the ground doesn't freeze); surround immediately with a watering basin.*
- **PLANT:** *In deep, well drained soil; at edge of lawns, not on hillsides or wet bottomlands.*

SPECIAL REQUIREMENTS: *Additional watering two weeks prior to harvest to bring nuts to full ripeness.*

HARVEST SEASON: *September to late November.*

COMMERCIAL AVAILABILITY: *Year round–unshelled, shelled, halves, chopped, ground, pieces*

SELECT: *Unshelled walnuts free of cracks; superior walnuts are well filled but have adequate space between the shell and the kernel; shelled should be plump, firm and meaty; shrivelled walnuts are past their prime. The skin is light–to dark–yellow, the kernel white. It turns grey with age.*

STORE: *Unshelled in a cool, dry place up to 3 months, (the French keep them in a wicker basket, never in the refrigerator); shelled should be refrigerated in airtight containers for up to 6 months; freeze up to a year. Dried walnuts will regain their flavor if soaked in milk overnight.*

NUTRITIONAL VALUE: *Walnuts are a good source of phosphorous and iron. They are high in vitamin C and contain vitamins A, B1, B2 and D.*

Dwayne Lindsay, a researcher at Diamond Walnut Growers in Stockton, CA, chews walnuts all day, every day, during the harvest. He determines each grade of walnut by its crunch.

Storing Nuts

Nuts are high in unsaturated fats and this richness makes them so appealing. Unfortunately, these fats break down or oxidize when exposed to heat, light, air and moisture.

Nuts can develop off-flavors and pick up surrounding odors unless stored properly. Nuts highest in fat, like macadamias and pecans are the most difficult to keep fresh.

Nuts stay fresher longer in their shells, about twice as long as shelled nuts, and whole nuts keep better than those chopped or ground. Unless vacuum-packed, nuts are best stored in a dark, cool, dry place in glass or plastic containers with tight-fitting lids. Store shelled nuts in the refrigerator or freeze in airtight bags.

Generally speaking nuts in the shell keep 4–7 months;
nuts (shelled) keep up to 1 year in the refrigerator;
nuts (shelled) keep up to 2 years frozen.

Cooking With Nuts

Always cook with the freshest nuts possible. Rancid nuts will ruin the flavor of any food. Buy nuts in small quantities and always taste first. Chopped or grated nuts stay dry and release flavor when the food is eaten. Nut pastes, made by grinding or crushing, allow the flavor of the nut to permeate the food as the oils are released.

- When adding nuts to meringue, choose nuts in the middle range of fat, such as almonds or filberts, since even the smallest amount of fat will stop egg whites from foaming.
- To remove shells, place nuts in a large saucepan and cover with water. Bring to a boil; remove from heat, cover and let stand 15 minutes. Dry and then crack with a nut cracker.
- To remove broken shells in hulled nuts, place in a bowl of water. Skim off shells that will float. Drain water and dry nuts.
- Nuts chop easier when warm. Heat 5 minutes in the oven at 325° F (160° C) or microwave on high for 1 minute. Chop 1 cup (250 ml) at a time in a food processor using quick on/off pulses to achieve desired texture. Don't overprocess. Adding a tablespoon (15 ml) of cornstarch or sugar (borrowed from the dry ingredients) will keep nuts from clumping during chopping or grinding by machine.

Oh God! I could be bounded in a nut shell, and count myself King of infinite space, were it not that I have bad dreams.

HAMLET

WILLIAM SHAKESPEARE

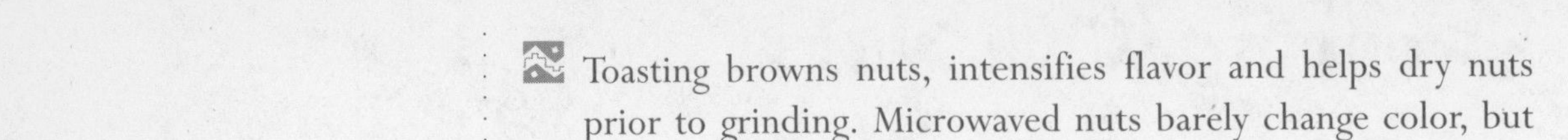

- Toasting browns nuts, intensifies flavor and helps dry nuts prior to grinding. Microwaved nuts barely change color, but taste toasted.
- Toasting intensifies flavor and helps keep nuts from sinking in batter-based foods. For best results, toast in a low over, 275° to 300° F (140° to 150° C) to avoid scorching. Turn nuts frequently until golden and watch carefully. Nuts will continue to become crisp and darken as they cool. Nuts may also be toasted in an ungreased frying pan. Use medium heat and stir frequently. To microwave, place 1 cup (250 ml) at a time on a paper plate. Microwave, uncovered, for 3–4 minutes on high. Rotate plate after 2 minutes.
- To remove skins pour boiling water over nuts and let stand one minute. Drain. Rub nuts between fingers or against the inside of a metal sieve to remove skins. Dry between paper towels.
- Substitute walnuts for pecans, hazelnuts for almonds or peanuts. Substitute ⅓ cup (75 ml) finely ground nuts for ⅓ cup (75 ml) flour to add flavor to baked goods. Press ¼ cup (50 ml) toasted, finely ground nuts into prepared, raw pastry shell.

 2 lbs unshelled nuts = approximately 1 lb shelled

 4 oz of most nuts = approximately 1 cup (250 ml) chopped nuts

THE Recipes

Nutty Butters, Snacks and Appetizers

Nutty Butters, Snacks and Appetizers

All nuts may be made into nut butter. They are best made using a food processor, as considerable processing (5 to 10 minutes depending upon the type of nut) is necessary to break down the nutmeat to a smooth consistency. Use raw, roasted, salted or unsalted nuts. Roasted nuts are more flavorful and whole nuts contain more natural oils than previously chopped ones. Purchase blanched (skinless) nuts, or follow earlier instructions for removing skins, as the skins take away from the smooth texture and some skins can be bitter.

Additional oil – preferably vegetable – is necessary to achieve a smooth, even consistency. The amount of oil will vary slightly, depending upon the type of nuts and their freshness. Add oil very gradually, checking for smoothness frequently. When making peanut butter, use half vegetable oil and half peanut oil. About 2 cups (500 ml) of nuts makes just over 1 cup (250 ml) of nut butter. Store in tightly sealed containers and refrigerate. Bring to room temperature before using and stir if oil has separated.

ALMOND BUTTER

2 cups (500 ml) blanched almonds
⅓ cup (75 ml) oil
salt to taste

Grind nuts to a fine powder in blender or food processor. Add oil and salt.

Refrigerate to store.

MAKES 1 CUP (250 ML).

CASHEW NUT BUTTER

2–4 Tbsp (30–60 ml) vegetable oil
1½ cups (375 ml) cashews
salt to taste

Process oil, nuts and salt in blender or food processor to desired consistency.

Brazil nuts, filberts, walnuts and pecans may be processed in the same fashion.

Refrigerate to store.

MAKES ¾ CUP (175 ML).

HAZELNUT BUTTER

¾ cup (175 ml) hazelnuts
2–3 Tbsp (30–45 ml) butter

- Place hazelnuts in a single layer on a cookie sheet and bake 15 minutes at 350° F (180° C).
- Place nuts on a clean towl and rub to remove skins; cool.
- Process nuts and butter in a blender or food processor to desired consistency.
- Refrigerate to store.

MAKES ½ CUP (125 ML).

PEANUT BUTTER

2 cups (500 ml) roasted skinless peanuts
1½ Tbsp (25 ml) peanut oil
1½ Tbsp (25 ml) vegetable oil
salt to taste
½ cup (125 ml) chopped roasted peanuts (optional)

- Place peanuts and peanut oil in food processor and process until smooth (several minutes).
- With processor running slowly, gradually add vegetable oil in a thin stream and salt. Test frequently for desired consistency.
- For crunchy peanut butter, stir in chopped peanuts.
- Refrigerate to store.

MAKES JUST OVER 1 CUP (250 ML).

Nutty snacks

These snacks may be packaged for gift giving. Be sure to cool before storing in airtight containers. They will keep at room temperature for several weeks.

SPICED ALMONDS

¼ cup (50 ml) butter
2 cups (500 ml) unblanched whole almonds (or peanuts)
1 Tbsp (15 ml) chili powder
1 large garlic clove, minced

- Melt butter in a skillet and add almonds, chili powder and minced garlic.
- Stir over medium heat until nuts are crisp and lightly browned.
- Remove from heat and sprinkle with salt.

MAKES 2 CUPS (500 ML).

VANILLA BEAN NUTS

1 lb (500 g) Brazil or macadamia nuts, shelled
3 Tbsp (45 ml) vegetable oil
3 Tbsp (45 ml) Cointreau
⅓ cup (75 ml) sugar
1 whole vanilla bean, pulverized in a blender
1 Tbsp (15 ml) cinnamon
1 tsp (5 ml) nutmeg
1 tsp (5 ml) cloves
salt to taste

- Blanch Brazil nuts in boiling water for 1 minute; drain and dry on paper towels; rub to remove skins.
- In a mixing bowl whisk oil, Cointreau and sugar; stir in nuts and let marinate 15 minutes.
- Spread nuts on a baking sheet and bake 2 minutes at 350° F (180° C).
- In a separate bowl combine vanilla bean and spices.
- Toss hot nuts in spice mixture, coating well.
- Sprinkle with salt.
- Spread nuts on paper towels to absorb excess oil while cooling.

MAKES 1 LB (500 G).

CURRIED CASHEWS

2 Tbsp (30 ml) butter
1 cup (250 ml) salted cashews
1 tsp (5 ml) curry powder

- Melt butter in a skillet.
- Add cashews and sprinkle with curry powder.
- Sauté until lightly browned.
- Cool on paper towels.

MAKES 1 CUP (250 ML).

MEXICAN PEANUTS

2 whole dried red or green chilies
4 cloves garlic, crushed
2 Tbsp (30 ml) olive oil
2 lbs (1 kg) blanched salted peanuts
salt to taste
1 tsp (5 ml) chili powder

- Chop chilies and cook in a skillet with garlic and oil over low heat for 1 minute.
- Add peanuts and continue cooking, stirring continuously.
- Remove from heat when peanuts are light brown.
- Add chili powder. Cool.

MAKES 2 LBS (1 KG).

SAVORY PEANUTS

¼ tsp (1 ml) garlic salt
2 tsp (10 ml) hot chili oil (available at Oriental markets)
3 Tbsp (45 ml) firmly packed brown sugar
3 Tbsp (45 ml) soy sauce
3 Tbsp (45 ml) cider vinegar
12 oz (340 g) dry roasted peanuts

In a mixing bowl combine all ingredients.

Line a baking sheet with foil and spray with non-stick cooking spray; spread nut mixture evenly on sheet.

Bake 20 minutes at 325° F (160° C), or until most of the liquid has evaporated, being careful not to burn.

Cool and store in airtight container.

MAKES 1½ CUPS (375 ML).

CURRIED PECANS

¼ cup (50 ml) sugar
1 tsp (5 ml) salt
1½ tsp (7 ml) curry powder
3½ cups (875 ml) pecan halves
¼ cup (50 ml) vegetable oil

In a mixing bowl combine sugar, salt and curry powder.

Place pecan halves on a baking sheet and sprinkle with oil and spice mixture.

Bake for 30 minutes, stirring every 10 minutes, at 275° (140° C).

Cool on paper towels.

MAKES 3½ CUPS (875 ML).

RUM PECANS

2 Tbsp (30 ml) butter
1 cup (250 ml) pecan halves
2 Tbsp (30 ml) dark rum
2 Tbsp (30 ml) soy sauce
½ tsp (2 ml) salt
2 drops hot pepper sauce

Melt butter in a skillet and cook pecan halves on low heat, stirring constantly until browned.

Stir in rum and simmer until liquid evaporates.

Add remaining ingredients and combine well.

Cool on paper towels.

MAKES 1 CUP (250 ML).

SPICY WALNUTS

2 Tbsp (30 ml) butter
4 cups (1 L) walnut halves
1½ Tbsp (25 ml) curry powder
1 Tbsp (15 ml) ground cumin
1½ tsp (7 ml) salt
½ tsp (2 ml) sugar

Melt butter in a skillet and add walnuts, sautéing 4 minutes on low heat, stirring frequently.
Add remaining ingredients, continuing to sauté and stir for several more minutes, until nuts are evenly coated.
Cool.

MAKES 4 CUPS (1 L).

SWEET WALNUTS

1 egg white
1 tsp (5 ml) water
¾ cup (175 ml) sugar
1 tsp (5 ml) salt
1½ tsp (7 ml) cinnamon
½ tsp (2 ml) ground cloves
½ tsp (2 ml) ground nutmeg
2 cups (500 ml) walnuts

In a mixing bowl beat egg white and water until stiff peaks form.
In another bowl combine sugar, salt and spices.
Pour nuts into egg white and toss to coat; then add to spice mixture and toss to coat.
Spread nuts on a greased baking sheet (nuts should be separated) and bake 30 minutes at 275° F (140° C).
Cool.

MAKES 2 CUPS (500 ML).

HOT MIXED NUTS

4 Tbsp (60 ml) butter
1 tsp (5 ml) seasoned salt
1 tsp (5 ml) pepper
1½ tsp (7 ml) cayenne pepper
1 tsp (5 ml) hot pepper sauce
1 cup (250 ml) whole almonds (blanched or skins on)
1 cup (250 ml) roasted peanuts
1 cup (250 ml) roasted cashews

Melt butter in a skillet and stir in seasoned salt, pepper, half the cayenne pepper, and the pepper sauce.

Add nuts and toss to coat.

Place nuts on a baking sheet and toast lightly for 20 minutes at 300° F (150° C), tossing after 10 minutes.

Add remainder of cayenne pepper. Cool.

MAKES 3 CUPS (750 ML).

HOMEMADE NUTS AND BOLTS

½ cup (125 ml) butter
1 Tbsp (15 ml) Worcestershire sauce
1 tsp (5 ml) celery salt
1 tsp (5 ml) onion salt
½ tsp (2 ml) garlic powder
⅛ tsp (.5 ml) garlic salt
3 cups (750 ml) round toasted oat cereal
2 cups (500 ml) bite-size wheat or bran square cereal
2 cups (500 ml) pretzel sticks
2 lbs (1 kg) peanuts or mixed nuts

In a saucepan melt butter and add Worcestershire sauce, and spices and mix well.

Place remaining ingredients in a roasting pan and add butter mixture, coating dry ingredients thoroughly.

Bake for 1½ to 2 hours at 200° F (100° C), stirring occasionally.

Cool and store in airtight containers.

MAKES ABOUT 12 CUPS (3 L).

GRANOLA

4½ cups (1 L, 125 ml) rolled oats
2 cups (500 ml) shredded coconut
¾ cup (175 ml) whole hazelnuts
¾ cup (175 ml) slivered almonds
6 Tbsp (90 ml) honey
¾ cup (175 ml) vegetable oil
½ cup (125 ml) golden raisins
½ cup (125 ml) dark raisins
1 cup (250 ml) chopped dates

Toss first four ingredients together and spread on a large baking sheet.

Blend honey and oil together and pour over oat mixture; stir until ingredients are coated.

Bake 40 minutes at 375° F (190° C) until golden brown.

Remove from oven and stir frequently until granola cools.

Stir in remaining ingredients and cool.

MAKES ABOUT 9 CUPS (2 L, 250 ML).

GRANOLA BARS

½ cup (125 ml) firmly packed brown sugar
½ cup (125 ml) light corn syrup
1 cup (250 ml) peanut butter
1 tsp (5 ml) vanilla
1½ cups (375 ml) quick-cooking oatmeal
1½ cups (375 ml) crisp rice cereal
1 cup (250 ml) raisins
½ cup (125 ml) flaked or shredded coconut
½ cup (125 ml) sunflower seeds
3 Tbsp (45 ml) sesame seeds

In a saucepan combine brown sugar and corn syrup and bring to a boil, stirring continuously.

Remove from heat and stir in peanut butter and vanilla.

Add remaining ingredients stirring until well mixed.

Press mixture into an ungreased 9-inch (22-cm) square pan.

Cool and cut into bars.

MAKES 20 BARS.

Appetizers

HOMEMADE CRACKERS

The irregular shape and bumpy texture of homemade crackers adds character to any hors d'oeuvre tray. The method of making crackers is similar to that of refrigerator cookies. The dough is formed into cylinders, wrapped tightly in plastic and chilled. It's important to use a sharp knife to slice the dough. Line baking sheets with parchment paper for easier clean-up. Crackers will store several weeks in airtight containers. To revive those that are less than crisp, bake 5 minutes at 275° F (140° C). Don't be afraid to experiment with flavored oils and vary the spices in these recipes.

PECAN CHEESE CRACKERS

1 lb (500 g) sharp cheddar cheese
½ lb (250 g) butter
pinch cayenne pepper
3 cups (750 ml) sifted flour
1 cup (250 ml) chopped pecans

In a mixing bowl cream cheese and butter. Add cayenne pepper and flour and mix thoroughly.

- Stir in pecans.
- Shape dough into logs about 1½ inches (4 cm) in diameter, cover and refrigerate overnight. (Dough may also be frozen.)
- Slice rolls ¼ inch (6 mm) thick with a sharp knife and bake on an ungreased baking sheet 12 to 15 minutes at 350° F (180° C).
- Cool.

MAKES ABOUT 60 CRACKERS.

GOAT CHEESE AND WALNUT CRACKERS

½ lb (250 g) goat cheese
8 Tbsp (120 ml) unsalted butter
2 Tbsp (30 ml) walnut oil
1⅓ cups (325 ml) flour
½ tsp (2 ml) thyme
¼ tsp (1 ml) salt
½ cup (125 ml) very finely chopped walnuts

- Cream cheese, butter and oil in a food processor.
- Add flour, thyme and salt and process until a doughy consistency.
- Add walnuts and process enough to blend.
- Shape dough into logs about 1½ inches (4 cm) in diameter, cover and refrigerate at least 2 hours.
- Slice rolls ¼ inch (6 mm) thick with a sharp knife and bake on an ungreased baking sheet, 15 minutes (until lightly browned around edges) at 350° F (180° C).
- Cool and store in airtight containers.

MAKES ABOUT 70 CRACKERS.

ALMOND SHRIMP TARTS

½ lb (500 g) raw shrimp (about 15), shelled, deveined and coarsely chopped
¼ cup (50 ml) chopped roasted almonds
1 cup (250 ml) heavy cream
2 Tbsp (30 ml) clam juice
2 eggs, lightly beaten
1 egg yolk, lightly beaten
⅛ tsp (.5 ml) grated nutmeg
salt to taste
1 dozen tart shells

- Combine all ingredients.
- Pour into tart shells and bake 25 to 30 minutes at 400° F (200° C).
- Cool 5 minutes before serving.

MAKES 12 TARTS.

CURRIED ALMOND-STUFFED BAGUETTE

1½ cups (375 ml) finely chopped cooked chicken
½ cup (125 ml) chopped blanched almonds
2 Tbsp (30 ml) grated coconut
1 Tbsp (15 ml) butter
1 Tbsp (15 ml) curry powder
2 Tbsp (30 ml) white wine
½ cup (125 ml) cream
2 egg yolks
1 baguette (French bread)

In a mixing bowl combine chicken, almonds and coconut and set aside.
In a saucepan melt butter and add curry powder blending well; mix in wine.
In a separate bowl combine cream and egg yolks and blend well, then add to wine mixture; stir several minutes, until thick.
Cool and add to chicken mixture.
Slice baguette lengthwise and hollow out the bread leaving shell about ½ inch (1 cm) thick.
Pack chicken mixture into hollow of baguette.
Place baguette halves together, wrap with plastic and refrigerate several hours.
Slice to serve.

MAKES 30 SLICES.

BRAZIL NUT CHEESE BALLS

3 oz (85 g) cream cheese
¼ cup (50 ml) crushed pineapple, well drained
¼ cup (50 ml) finely chopped Brazil nuts

Beat cream cheese until smooth and add pineapple.
Form into ½ inch (12 mm) balls and roll in Brazil nuts.
Cover and refrigerate until serving.

MAKES 24 BALLS.

BRAZILIAN EGGS

6 hard-cooked eggs
½ cup (125 ml) finely chopped Brazil nuts
2 tsp (10 ml) vinegar
⅛ tsp (.5 ml) dry mustard
½ tsp (2 ml) salt
½ tsp (2 ml) Worcestershire sauce
⅛ tsp (.5 ml) Tabasco sauce
2 Tbsp (30 ml) mayonnaise

Halve eggs and remove yolks, mashing with a fork.
Add remaining ingredients to yolks and fill egg halves.
Cover and refrigerate until serving.

MAKES 12 HALVES.

COCONUT CHICKEN FINGERS

¾ cup (175 ml) flour
¼ tsp (1 ml) salt, pepper
1 lb (500 g) chicken breasts, skined, deboned and cut into 1-inch (2.5-cm) strips

BATTER

1 cup (250 ml) flour
½ tsp (2 ml) salt
½ tsp (2 ml) baking soda
1 cup (250 ml) beer

BREADING

2¼ cups (550 ml) shredded coconut
1¾ cups (425 ml) coarse, dried white bread crumbs (Panko brand Japanese-style bread crumbs found in Oriental markets are best)
oil for frying

In a shallow bowl combine flour, salt and pepper and set aside.
In a separate bowl whisk batter ingredients.
In a third bowl combine coconut and bread crumbs.
Heat oil to 350° F (180° C).
Dredge chicken strips in flour mixture, drop in batter and coat with coconut breading. Drop into hot oil and cook 3 to 4 minutes, until golden brown. Serve with chutney or plum sauce.

MAKES 6 SERVINGS.

COCONUT SHRIMP

½ cup (125 ml) flour
pinch salt
pinch paprika
pepper to taste
½ cup (125 ml) beer
1 lb (500 g) raw shrimp (about 25), shells removed and deveined
1 cup (250 ml) shredded coconut
vegetable oil

In a bowl combine flour, salt, paprika and pepper. Stir in beer and mix to the consistency of pancake batter.
Coat each shrimp with batter and dredge in coconut.
In a skillet heat oil until hot. Fry shrimp until brown on all sides.
Remove shrimps with a slotted spoon and drain excess fat on paper towels.
Serve immediately.

MAKES 25 SHRIMP.

MACADAMIA BALL

16 oz (500 g) cream cheese, softened
1½ cups (375 ml) grated cheddar cheese
2 tsp (10 ml) minced onion
½ cup (125 ml) chopped sweet pickles
1 tsp (5 ml) salt
½ cup (125 ml) chopped macadamias

- In a bowl combine cheeses, onion, pickels and salt.
- Shape into a ball and roll in macadamias.
- Cover and refrigerate several hours.
- Serve at room temperature with crackers.

MAKES 4 CUPS (1 L) OR A LARGE BALL.

SHERRY PECAN CHEESE LOG

3 Tbsp (45 ml) sherry (or brandy)
½ cup (125 ml) soft butter
⅔ cup (150 ml) crumbled blue cheese
4 oz (125 g) cream cheese
2 Tbsp (30 ml) grated Parmesan cheese
3 drops Tabasco sauce
4 oz (125 g) finely chopped pecans

- In a food processor combine sherry and butter.
- Gradually add remaining ingredients except pecans and blend until smooth.
- Shape mixture into a log.
- Roll in pecans, cover and refrigerate.
- Serve at room temperature with crackers.

MAKES 1½ CUPS (375 ML) OR ONE LOG.

PECAN CHEESE ROUNDS

1 cup (250 ml) butter
1 cup (250 ml) grated old cheddar cheese
2½ cups (625 ml) all-purpose flour
1 tsp (5 ml) salt
½ tsp (2 ml) cayenne pepper
1 cup (250 ml) finely chopped pecans

- In a food processor combine butter and cheese well.
- Work in flour, salt, cayenne pepper and nuts.
- Chill thoroughly.
- Divide dough into 4 rolls and chill again.
- Slice into thin rounds the size of a medal.
- Bake 10 minutes at 400° F (200° C). May be frozen.

MAKES 100 ROUNDS.

PISTACHIO CHICKEN BALLS

½ cup (125 ml) shelled coarsely chopped pistachio nuts, divided in half
1½ cups (375 ml) cooked chicken
2 Tbsp (30 ml) olive oil
1 Tbsp (15 ml) lemon juice
salt
fresh ground pepper

- In a food processor combine half the pistachios and the chicken.
- Add oil, lemon juice, salt and pepper to taste.
- Roll in bite-size balls and roll in remaining pistachios.

MAKES 3 DOZEN BALLS.

PESTO BRIE

2 cups (500 ml) loosely packed basil leaves
3 Tbsp (45 ml) toasted pine nuts
1 clove garlic
1 Tbsp (15 ml) olive oil
½ tsp (2 ml) ground pepper
2 lb (1 kg) wheel of Brie cheese, well chilled

- In a food processor combine basil, pine nuts, garlic, oil and pepper until smooth.
- Slice wheel of Brie in half horizontally.
- Spread pesto mixture evenly on bottom half of cheese wheel.
- Replace top half, wrap and refrigerate for 1 to 2 days.
- Serve at room temperature with crackers.

MAKES ABOUT 32 SERVINGS.

STUFFED MUSHROOMS

3 Tbsp (45 ml) sour cream
3 Tbsp (45 ml) cream cheese
⅛ tsp (.5 ml) curry powder
12 whole mushrooms
12 walnut halves

- Clean mushrooms and remove stems.
- Combine sour cream and cream cheese.
- Add curry powder to taste.
- Fill mushroom caps with cream mixture and garnish each with a walnut half.
- Refrigerate until serving.

MAKES 12 MUSHROOMS.

HAM AND PISTACHIO-STUFFED BAGUETTE

2 cups (500 ml) packed spinach leaves
4 oz (125 g) cream cheese
¼ cup (50 ml) fresh dill
1 Tbsp (15 ml) cream
4 cups (1 L) minced ham
⅓ cup (75 ml) toasted unsalted coarsely chopped pistachios
⅓ cup (75 ml) mayonnaise
1 Tbsp (15 ml) Dijon mustard
1 baguette (French bread)

Clean and cook spinach in a small amount of water just until wilted, about 3 minutes; drain and pat dry with paper towels, then chop fine.

In a food processor combine spinach, cream cheese, and dill and cream until smooth. Do not over process.

In a mixing bowl combine ham, nuts, mayonnaise and mustard.

Slice baguette lengthwise and hollow out the bread, leaving shell about ½ inch (1 cm) thick.

Coat inside of baguette with cheese mixture, especially around edges to seal.

Pack ham mixture into hollow of baguette.

Place baguette halves together, wrap in plastic and refrigerate several hours.

Slice to serve.

MAKES 30 SLICES.

GORGONZOLA AND WALNUT DIP

½ lb (250 g) Gorgonzola cheese
½ lb (250 g) cream cheese
½ cup (125 ml) heavy cream
⅓ cup (75 ml) chopped walnuts
2 tsp (10 ml) cognac

In a food processor combine cheeses and heavy cream.

Fold in walnuts and cognac with a spoon.

Chill several hours.

Serve at room temperature with crackers or vegetables.

MAKES 2½ CUPS (625 ML).

POTTED BLACK WALNUT CHEESE

1⅓ cups (325 ml) shredded cheddar cheese
1⅓ cups (325 ml) shredded Monterey Jack cheese
6 Tbsp (90 ml) unsalted butter, softened
2 Tbsp (60 ml) white wine (or dry sherry or vermouth)
pinch mace
½ cup (125 ml) black walnuts, chopped medium-fine

- Cream the cheeses and butter together.
- Beat in wine and mace.
- Stir in black walnuts.
- Pack into serving dishes.
- Cover and refrigerate until ready to serve.

Keeps several weeks or may be frozen.

- Serve at room temperature with crackers.

MAKES 3 CUPS (625 ML).

Soups, Salads, Dressings and Sauces

Almond cream soup

3 Tbsp (45 ml) almond paste
⅔ cup (150 ml) chopped almonds
2 qts (2.5 L) chicken broth
3 egg yolks, lightly beaten
2 cups (500 ml) heavy cream
½ tsp (2 ml) sugar
¼ tsp (1 ml) almond extract
slivered almonds

In a large saucepan blend almond paste, chopped almonds and broth; bring to a boil, then lower heat and simmer 30 minutes.
In a mixing bowl beat egg yolks, cream, and sugar.
Dilute with some of the hot broth; add mixture to hot broth and whisk to blend.
Continue to cook slowly, stirring constantly until thick. Add almond extract.
Garnish with slivered amonds and serve immediately

Makes 8 servings.

Almond and pine nut soup

¾ cup (175 ml) blanched almonds
½ cup (125 ml) pine nuts
½ cup (125 ml) sugar
3⅓ cups (825 ml) whole milk
1½ tsp (7 ml) cinnamon

Soak nuts in warm water for 1 hour; drain, add sugar and grind until fine in food processor.
In a saucepan combine nuts and milk and bring to a boil; remove from heat.
Serve hot garnished with cinnamon.

Makes 4 servings.

Cashew and mushroom soup

3 Tbsp (45 ml) butter
3 Tbsp (45 ml) flour
1½ cups (375 ml) chicken broth
1½ cups (375 ml) 10% cream

nutmeg, pepper to taste
2 Tbsp (30 ml) butter
2 cups (500 ml) sliced mushrooms
¾ cup (175 ml) coarsely chopped cashews
whole cashews for garnish

- In a saucepan melt butter and stir in flour.
- Add chicken broth, cream and spices, stirring continuously until mixture thickens.
- Sauté mushrooms in melted butter and add to soup mixture; stir in chopped cashews.
- Serve hot garnished with whole cashews.

Makes 4 servings.

Traditional chestnut soup

3 Tbsp (45 ml) butter
13 oz (390 g) whole peeled chestnuts
⅓ cup (75 ml) chopped onion
½ cup (125 ml) chopped celery
3½ cups (875 ml) chicken broth
1 small carrot, peeled and sliced
¼ cup (50 ml) red wine
salt, pepper, nutmeg to taste

- In a skillet melt 2 Tbsp (30 ml) of butter and sauté chestnuts for 10 minutes.
- In a large pot, sauté onion and celery in remaining butter until tender.
- Add broth to the onion mixture and bring to a boil.
- Add carrot and chestnuts and simmer 15 minutes.
- Add wine and simmer 15 minutes.
- Purée soup in food processor and return to pot.
- Add salt, pepper and nutmeg to taste.
- Simmer 10–15 minutes, stirring frequently.

Makes 10 to 12 servings.

Hazelnut soup

3 Tbsp (45 ml) butter, melted
1 cup (250 ml) diced celery
1 cup (250 ml) diced onion
4 Tbsp (60 ml) flour
1 tsp (5 ml) salt
¾ tsp (3 ml) Worcestershire sauce
pepper to taste
2 cups (500 ml) milk
2 cups (500 ml) chicken broth
½ cup (125 ml) ground hazelnuts
½ cup (125 ml) chopped hazelnuts

In a skillet melt butter and sauté celery and onion.

Stir in flour, salt, Worcestershire sauce and pepper.

Add milk, broth, and ground hazelnuts; simmer 10 to 15 minutes.

Serve hot garnished with chopped hazelnuts.

MAKES 4 TO 6 SERVINGS.

PEANUT SOUP

2 Tbsp (30 ml) butter
2 Tbsp (30 ml) finely chopped onion
¼ cup (50 ml) thinly sliced celery
2 Tbsp (30 ml) flour
3 cups (750 ml) chicken broth
½ cup (125 ml) peanut butter
¼ tsp (1 ml) salt
2 tsp (10 ml) lemon juice
2 Tbsp (30 ml) chopped roasted peanuts

In a saucepan melt butter and add onions and celery; sauté 5 minutes.

Add flour and mix until blended.

Stir in broth and simmer 30 minutes.

Remove from heat and strain.

Stir peanut butter, salt and lemon juice into strained broth and mix well.

Serve hot garnished with chopped peanuts.

MAKES 6 SERVINGS.

WALNUT SOUP

1½ cups (375 ml) 10% cream
½ cup (125 ml) ground walnuts
2 Tbsp (30 ml) butter
1 onion, finely chopped
2 Tbsp (30 ml) flour
3 cups (750 ml) chicken broth
salt, pepper to taste
2 egg yolks
toasted croutons

In a saucepan scald half the cream and add nuts; turn off heat and let stand while preparing other ingredients.

In a skillet melt butter and sauté onion.

Stir in flour; add broth and seasonings.

Simmer 10 minutes; add walnut mixture.

Beat egg yolks and remaining cream together; heat with some of the broth mixture, then add to soup.

Cook on low heat, stirring constantly until thick.

Serve immediately garnished with croutons.

MAKES 4 SERVINGS.

Salad dressings and salads

ALMOND GARLIC DRESSING

⅛ cup (25 ml) toasted blanched almonds
4 garlic cloves
1 chili pepper, seeded, or ¼ tsp (1 ml) cayenne pepper
¼ cup (50 ml) olive oil
2 Tbsp (30 ml) wine vinegar
½ tsp (2 ml) salt

In a food processor combine almonds and garlic.

Add chili pepper and blend well.

With food processor running slowly, add oil in a thin stream until blended.

Add vinegar and salt; blend thoroughly.

MAKES ½ CUP (125 ML).

HAZELNUT BLUE CHEESE DRESSING

¼ cup (50 ml) buttermilk
2 eggs
2 tsp (10 ml) white wine vinegar
1 garlic clove
½ tsp (2 ml) salt
pinch pepper
pinch cayenne pepper
1½ cups (375 ml) olive oil
¼ cup (50 ml) crumbled blue cheese
¼ cup (50 ml) hazelnuts, toasted and chopped
⅛ tsp (.5 ml) chopped parsley
¼ tsp (1 ml) lemon zest

In a food processor combine buttermilk, eggs, vinegar, garlic, salt and peppers until well mixed.

With food processor running slowly, add oil in a thin stream. When creamy, add blue cheese, hazelnuts, parsley and lemon zest. Refrigerate until use.

MAKES 2 CUPS (500 ML).

PEANUT DRESSING

½ cup (125 ml) olive oil
2 Tbsp (30 ml) rice vinegar
2 Tbsp (30 ml) finely chopped peanuts
2 Tbsp (30 ml) toasted sesame seeds
3 green onions, finely chopped (including greens)
½ tsp (2 ml) pepper
1 garlic, minced

- In a small bowl combine all ingredients.
- Refrigerate until use; keeps several days.

MAKES ½ CUP (125 ML).

WALNUT DRESSING

1 Tbsp (15 ml) diced raw bacon
1 tsp (5 ml) diced onion
1 tsp (5 ml) sugar
3 Tbsp (45 ml) toasted walnuts
2 Tbsp (30 ml) cider vinegar
1 Tbsp (15 ml) walnut oil
3 Tbsp (45 ml) salad oil
salt, pepper to taste

- Sauté bacon and onion and drain off fat.
- Combine bacon, onion, sugar and walnuts and purée in a blender with remaining ingredients.
- Warm slightly before tossing with salad.

MAKES ½ CUP (125 ML).

ORANGE WALNUT DRESSING

⅓ cup (75 ml) walnut oil
juice of 1 large orange
juice of half a lemon
pinch ground nutmeg

- In a bowl whisk oil and juices until blended.
- Add nutmeg.

MAKES ½ CUP (125 ML).

SALAD ALICE

6 large, ripe eating apples with stems
1 lemon, cut in half
1⅓ cups (325 ml) red seedless grapes, halved
1⅓ cups (325 ml) chopped blanched almonds
½ cup (125 ml) heavy cream
salt to taste
lettuce

- Slice the tops off the apples leaving stems intact; rub exposed apple tops with lemon.
- With a paring knife carefully hollow out flesh from apples so that the apples can be diced and the shell will still stand (about ¼ inch (6 mm) thick); rub interiors with lemon.
- Discard cores and seeds and dice remaining apple.
- Combine apple with grapes and nuts.

Just before serving, squeeze juice from lemon and combine with cream and salt.

Add cream to fruit and fill apples, placing lids on top.

Serve on lettuce.

MAKES 6 SERVINGS.

ALMOND SHRIMP WALDORF SALAD

DRESSING

1 egg
juice of half a lemon
¾ tsp (4 ml) Dijon mustard
¼ tsp (1 ml) chopped garlic
¾ tsp (4 ml) white vinegar
½ cup (125 ml) vegetable oil
¾ tsp (4 ml) fresh ground pepper
salt to taste
¼ cup (50 ml) whipping cream

In a food processor blend egg, lemon juice, mustard, garlic and vinegar until well combined.

With machine running slowly add oil in a thin stream until blended.

Add salt, pepper and cream.

MAKES ABOUT ¾ CUP (175 ML).

SALAD

2 Granny Smith apples, cut in chunks
juice of a lemon
½ cup (125 ml) white wine
1 sweet onion, cut in chunks
½ cup (125 ml) bacon cut in ½-inch (1.2-cm) pieces and fried until brown
½ cup (125 ml) celery, cut in chunks
¼ cup (50 ml) chopped scallions
½ Tbsp (7 ml) butter
1 clove garlic, chopped
pinch salt
fresh ground pepper to taste
1 cup (250 ml) raw shrimps (about 18), peeled and deveined
½ cup (125 ml) toasted slivered almonds

In a bowl toss apples with half the lemon juice; add wine and let stand 30 minutes.

Drain apples and discard wine.

Add onions, bacon, celery and scallions and refrigerate.

In a skillet melt butter over medium heat and cook garlic, until soft, in salt, pepper and remaining lemon juice. Add shrimp and cook until opaque. Allow to cool in pan then add shrimp, along with pan drippings to salad.

Toss salad with dressing and almonds.

MAKES 6 SERVINGS.

CUCUMBER CASHEW SALAD

2 medium cucumbers
1 tsp (5 ml) oil
½ tsp (2 ml) mustard seed
½ tsp (2 ml) cumin seed
½ cup (125 ml) plain low-fat yogurt
⅛ tsp (.5 ml) tumeric
⅛ tsp (.5 ml) cayenne pepper
⅛ tsp (.5 ml) pepper
2 tsp (10 ml) minced cilantro
½ cup (125 ml) coarsely chopped cashews

- Peel cucumbers, cut in half lengthwise, remove seeds and cut into thin slices.
- In a skillet heat oil and toast the mustard and cumin seeds until they begin to pop (2 minutes).
- Combine seeds with remaining ingredients, except cucumbers and cashews.
- Add cucumbers and cashews and chill before serving.

MAKES 4 SERVINGS.

CHESTNUT POTATO SALAD

20 whole tiny new potatoes
2 Tbsp (30 ml) butter
6 scallions, chopped
¼ cup (50 ml) white wine
1 cup (250 ml) whole cooked chestnuts
½ tsp (2 ml) dill
¼ cup (50 ml) salad oil
salt, pepper to taste
1 tsp (5 ml) parsley

- Boil potatoes until tender; drain and add butter while hot.
- Toss in remaining ingredients except parsley.
- Refrigerate 4 hours.
- Garnish with parsley before serving.

MAKES 6 SERVINGS.

MACADAMIA SWEET POTATO SALAD

½ lb (250 g) bacon cut in small pieces
3 cups (750 ml) sweet potatoes, cooked and diced
2 cups (500 ml) fresh pineapple chunks
½ cup (125 ml) mayonnaise

1 Tbsp (15 ml) Dijon mustard
pepper to taste
romaine lettuce
½ cup (125 ml) macadamias

In a skillet fry bacon until crisp and drain on paper towels.
In a large bowl toss sweet potatoes and pineapple.
In a small bowl combine mayonnaise, mustard and pepper and add to sweet potato mixture. Chill.
Stir in nuts just before serving.

MAKES 6 SERVINGS.

PEANUT SHRIMP SALAD

3 cups (750 ml) cooked rice, cooled
1 lb (500 g) cooked shrimp
2 hard-cooked eggs, diced
2 large tomatoes, cut in wedges
1 cup chopped roasted peanuts
¼ cup (50 ml) lemon juice
¼ cup (50 ml) finely chopped green pepper

DRESSING

½ cup (125 ml) peanut oil
⅛ cup (30 ml) white vinegar
⅛ cup (30 ml) lemon juice
1 clove garlic, minced
¼ tsp (1 ml) oregano
¼ tsp (1 ml) pepper

Toss salad ingredients in a salad bowl.
In a jar with a lid combine dressing ingredients and shake vigorously; let stand 15 minutes before using.
Toss salad with dressing.

MAKES 6 SERVINGS.

CRANBERRY PECAN SALAD MOLD

4 3-oz (85-g) packages black raspberry Jello
1 envelope unflavored gelatin
2 cups (500 ml) boiling water
½ cup (125 ml) cold water
2 cups (500 ml) fresh cranberries
2 oranges, peeled and seeded
2 apples, unpeeled but cored
1 14-oz (250-ml) can crushed pineapple, undrained
1 cup (250 ml) pecans
2 cups (500 ml) sugar
1 tsp (5 ml) mayonnaise

Dissolve Jello and gelatin in boiling water; add cold water and refrigerate until partially firm.

In a food processor combine fruits and pecans until coarsely chopped.

Stir in sugar until it dissolves.

Add mixture to gelatin, combine and pour into a 10-cup (2-L) ring mold that has been greased with 1 tsp (5 ml) of mayonnaise.

Refrigerate until firm.

Release mold onto a bed of lettuce.

MAKES 16 TO 20 SERVINGS.

PINE NUT SALAD

¼ cup (50 ml) pine nuts
1 head romaine lettuce
4 oz (125 g) feta cheese, crumbled
½ cup (125 ml) seedless grapes, halved
pinch salt
3 Tbsp (45 ml) white wine vinegar
½ cup (125 ml) olive oil
fresh ground pepper

In a skillet brown pine nuts until golden, about 2 minutes, stirring constantly; set aside.

Tear lettuce into bite-size pieces and combine with pine nuts, cheese and grapes.

In a small bowl whisk salt and vinegar.

Whisk in olive oil and pepper.

Toss with salad.

MAKES 4–6 SERVINGS.

PISTACHIO RICE SALAD

4 cups (1 L) cooked rice, cooled
2 cups (500 ml) diced cooked chicken
½ cup (125 ml) mayonnaise
juice of half a lemon
3 green onions, chopped
⅔ cup (150 ml) shelled and coarsely chopped pistachios
½ tsp (2 ml) tarragon
pepper to taste
10 oz (285 ml) mandarin oranges, drained

Combine all ingredients.

Chill and serve on lettuce.

MAKES 6–8 SERVINGS.

GREEN BEAN WALNUT SALAD

2 lbs (1 kg) baby green beans
¾ cup (175 ml) chopped walnuts
½ cup (125 ml) thinly sliced mushrooms
salt, pepper to taste
1 Tbsp (15 ml) Dijon mustard
½ cup (125 ml) walnut oil (olive oil)
¼ cup (50 ml) tarragon vinegar
2 Tbsp (30 ml) chopped fresh parsley

In a large pot or steamer cook beans until tender; drain and rinse with cold water and drain again.

Place beans in a salad bowl and sprinkle with walnuts and mushrooms.

In a small bowl combine remaining ingredients except parsley.

Pour dressing over salad; toss and garnish with parsley.

MAKES 6 SERVINGS.

WALNUT AND WILD RICE SALAD

2 qt (2.5 L) water
1½ tsp (7 ml) salt
1⅔ cups (400 ml) wild rice
¼ cup (50 ml) red wine vinegar
½ cup (125 ml) olive oil
3 scallions, chopped
½ cup (125 ml) toasted walmuts
1 orange
1 cup (250 ml) seedless red grapes, halved
1 tsp (5 ml) fresh ground pepper

In a large saucepan bring water to a boil; add ½ tsp (2 ml) salt and rice; cover and simmer 35 minutes until rice is tender but chewy.

Drain well and place rice in a large salad bowl.

Add vinegar, oil and scallions and mix well.

Chop walnuts in coarse pieces and add to salad.

Remove the orange zest with a grater and add to salad; peel and cut the orange into bite-size pieces and add to salad.

Toss in grapes and season with remaining salt and pepper.

MAKES 6–8 SERVINGS.

BEET AND ROQUEFORT SALAD WITH WALNUTS

8 medium-sized beets
3 Tbsp (45 ml) red wine vinegar
3 Tbsp (45 ml) walnut oil
½ cup (125 ml) walnut halves
¼ lb (125 g) Roquefort cheese
pepper to taste

Wash and trim beets and boil in salted water until tender; drain, cool, peel and cut into matchstick-size pieces.
In a mixing bowl toss beets with vinegar and walnut oil to coat; cover and chill.
When ready to serve, toss chilled beets with walnuts and bring to room temperature.
Crumble Roquefort cheese over salad and season with pepper.

MAKES 6–8 SERVINGS.

WALDORF SALAD

1 cup (250 ml) diced celery
1 cup (250 ml) diced apples, sprinkled with lemon juice to prevent browning
1 cup (250 ml) seedless grapes, halved
½ cup (125 ml) walnuts (or pecans)
¾ cup (175 ml) mayonnaise

Toss fruits and nuts; combine with mayonnaise.
Chill and serve cold in lettuce cups.

MAKES 4–6 SERVINGS.

WALNUT AND WATERCRESS SALAD

1 cup (250 ml) walnut halves
1 bunch of watercress, tough stems removed
1 apple, peeled, cored and diced
¼ cup (50 ml) Gruyère cheese, diced
2 tsp (10 ml) finely chopped Spanish onion
8 ripe olives

VINAIGRETTE

½ cup (125 ml) walnut oil
1 Tbsp (15 ml) red wine vinegar
½ tsp (2 ml) Dijon mustard
salt, pepper to taste

Place salad ingredients in a salad bowl.
In a small bowl combine dressing ingredients.
Pour over salad, toss and serve immediately.

MAKES 4 SERVINGS.

Savory sauces

ROMESCO SAUCE

5 oz (140 g) whole almonds, blanched or skins on, unsalted
3 red peppers
3 garlic cloves, coarsely chopped
1 Tbsp (15 ml) chopped fresh parsley
½ tsp (2 ml) salt
¼ tsp (1 ml) fresh ground pepper
2 Tbsp (30 ml) red wine vinegar
¾ cup (175 ml) fruity olive oil
pinch hot chili peppers (or cayenne)

- In a food processor grind nuts until fine.
- Cut peppers in half, remove seeds and place on a baking sheet with skin side up; bake at 400° F (200° C) until skins blister.
- Remove from oven and peel skins.
- In a food processor combine peppers, garlic, parsley salt and pepper; when well blended add nuts and vinegar and continue to process.
- With food processor running slowly, add oil in a thin stream until well blended.
- Add chili peppers and continue to blend.
- Serve with pasta poached chicken, rice, baked potatoes, or use in place of mayonnaise.

MAKES JUST UNDER 2 CUPS (500 ML).

SPANISH ROMESCO SAUCE

1 sweet red pepper
10 hazelnuts
10 almonds
4 garlic cloves
3 medium tomatoes
1 Tbsp (15 ml) chopped parsley
2 Tbsp (30 ml) wine vinegar
5 Tbsp (75 ml) olive oil
salt, pepper to taste

- Cut pepper in half, remove seeds and place on a baking sheet skin side up with nuts, garlic and tomatoes; bake at 400° F (200° C).
- Remove nuts when brown, garlic and tomatoes when soft and pepper when the skin has blistered (about 25 minutes in total).
- In a blender or food processor purée nuts, garlic and pepper; add tomatoes and parsley and blend well.
- Add vinegar, oil, salt and pepper.
- Leave at room temperature at least 2 hours before serving.
- Serve with pasta poached chicken, rice, baked potatoes, or use in place of mayonnaise.

MAKES ABOUT 1 CUP (250 ML).

CASHEW CHUTNEY

1 cup (250 ml) raw cashews
2 Tbsp (30 ml) jalapeno or chili peppers, seeded, coarsely chopped
¼ cup (50 ml) finely chopped peeled ginger root
¼ cup (50 ml) chopped fresh parsley leaves
½ tsp (2 ml) salt
juice of 1 lemon

In a blender or food processor grind nuts to make a paste.

Add peppers, ginger and parsley and continue to process.

Add salt and lemon juice and combine well. Mixture should be the consistency of mayonnaise.

Refrigerate until ready to serve.

Serve as a dip for raw vegetables, a sauce for fish or a substitute for mayonnaise.

MAKES 1½ CUPS (375 ML).

HAZELNUT SATAY

1 cup (250 ml) hazelnuts, toasted and puréed
1 Tbsp (15 ml) vegetable oil
⅔ cup (150 ml) water
2 Tbsp (30 ml) lime juice
2½ Tbsp (40 ml) soy sauce
2 tsp (10 ml) red pepper flakes
1 garlic clove
1 Tbsp (15 ml) lemon juice

Combine all ingredients until well blended. Refrigerate until use. Thin with water if sauce becomes too thick.

Serve as a dip for cheese, vegetables, chicken wings, pork or fish.

MAKES 1½ CUPS (375 ML).

HAZELNUT MUSHROOM SAUCE

¼ cup (50 ml) butter
1 onion, chopped
1 cup (250 ml) sliced mushrooms
1 garlic clove, chopped
1 cup (250 ml) chopped hazelnuts
1 Tbsp (15 ml) flour
1 cup (250 ml) chicken or vegetable stock

1 Tbsp (15 ml) white wine vinegar
1 Tbsp (15 ml) white wine
⅛ tsp (.5 ml) cinnamon
⅛ tsp (.5 ml) allspice
⅛ tsp (.5 ml) nutmeg
salt to taste
pepper to taste

In a heavy skillet melt butter and sauté onions, mushrooms, garlic and hazelnuts until onions are clear and nuts are toasted.
Sprinkle flour over mixture and stir 3 minutes.
Add chicken stock, vinegar, wine, spices and salt and pepper to taste.
Cook until sauce is thick and smooth.
Serve over rice, vegetables or poached meats.

MAKES 3 CUPS (750 ML).

INDONESIAN PEANUT SAUCE

1 Tbsp (15 ml) peanut oil
1 lb (500 g) onions, finely chopped
1 garlic clove, chopped
1 tsp (5 ml) ground cumin
½ tsp (2 ml) ground ginger
¾ cup (175 ml) peanut butter
2 Tbsp (30 ml) coconut cream
chili powder, salt to taste

In a heavy skillet heat oil and add onions, garlic and spices; stir well and reduce heat.
Add peanut butter and coconut cream; cover and simmer 2–3 hours stirring occasionally (add water if necessary to keep from sticking).
When sauce is thick add chili powder and salt to taste and cook another 10 minutes.
Serve with satay, rice or vegetables.

MAKES ABOUT ½ CUP (125 ML).

THAI PEANUT SAUCE

⅔ cup (150 ml) crunchy peanut butter
1½ cups (375 ml) coconut milk
2 Tbsp (30 ml) soy sauce
¼ cup (50 ml) lemon juice
2 tsp (10 ml) brown sugar
4 cloves garlic, minced
salt to taste
cayenne pepper to taste
¼ cup (50 ml) chicken stock
¼ cup (50 ml) whipping cream

In a saucepan combine first eight ingredients; stir constantly over low heat until smooth and thick.
Place in a blender and purée briefly.
Add stock and cream and blend until smooth.

May be refrigerated several hours until use.

Serve over Thai noodles, pasta, cold poached chicken or vegetables.

MAKES ABOUT 2½ CUPS (625 ML).

PINE NUT SAUCE

¼ cup (50 ml) butter
½ cup (125 ml) pine nuts, sliced
2 Tbsp (30 ml) lemon juice

In a saucepan melt butter and add pine nuts, cooking slowly for 5 minutes, until butter browns slightly.

Add lemon juice and heat.

Serve with fish.

MAKES 6 SERVINGS.

GADO GADO DIP

1 oz (30 g) dried tamarind pulp (available at Oriental or Indian markets)
½ cup (125 ml) boiling water
1½ Tbsp (25 ml) finely chopped onions
½ tsp (2 ml) finely chopped garlic
½ tsp (2 ml) shrimp paste (trassi; available at Oriental or Indian markets)
⅔ cup (150 ml) water
1 cup (250 ml) finely ground unsalted peanuts
¾ Tbsp (12 ml) brown sugar
¾ tsp (3 ml) finely chopped fresh chili peppers
1 bay leaf
¼ tsp (1 ml) finely grated fresh ginger root
1 cup (250 ml) unsweetened coconut milk

In a small bowl place tamarind pulp and cover with boiling water; stir occasionally, letting soak for about 1 hour, until pulp dissolves.

Rub tamarind through a fine sieve, pressing hard with the back of a spoon; discard seeds and fibers and retain tamarind water, refrigerating until use.

In a heavy skillet heat oil over moderate heat until a haze forms; add onions and garlic and stir frequently until soft, about 5 minutes.

Add shrimp paste and blend with onions.

Pour in water and bring to a boil on high.

Sitr in peanuts, brown sugar, chilies, bay leaf, ginger root and salt.

Reduce heat to low and add coconut milk and ⅛ cup (25 ml) tamarind water.

Simmer 15 minutes or until sauce is thick, stirring occasionally.

Remove bay leaf before serving.

Serve with rice or vegetable dishes.

MAKES ABOUT 2 CUPS (500 ML).

Pasta, Vegetables and Stuffings

Angel hair with almond sauce

½ cup (125 ml) slivered almonds
¼ cup (50 ml) olive oil
½ cup (125 ml) packed fresh parsley leaves
¼ cup (50 ml) packed fresh basil leaves
2 garlic cloves, chopped
½ tsp (2 ml) salt
1 lb (500 g) angel hair pasta
¼ cup (50 ml) sun-dried tomatoes, finely chopped
fresh ground pepper to taste
Parmesan cheese to taste

Spread almonds on a baking sheet and toast in the oven until brown.

Combine half the almonds with oil, parsley, basil, garlic and salt and process in a blender or food processor.

Boil angel hair until *al dente*. Drain and toss with remaining almonds, almond mixture and sun-dried tomatoes.

Garnished with pepper and Parmesan cheese and serve immediately.

Makes 4 servings.

Fusilli with seared shrimp in coconut milk curry

1½ Tbsp (25 ml) unsalted butter
1 onion, peeled and diced
1 small carrot, peeled and diced
1 stalk celery, diced
1 Tbsp (15 ml) medium curry powder
1 13-oz (390-ml) tin coconut milk
2 Tbsp (30 ml) vegetable oil (not olive oil)
1 lb (500 g) raw shrimp (about 25) shells removed and deveined
salt and pepper to taste
6 oz (170 g) snow peas, ends removed and cut into thin strips
1 Tbsp (15 ml) fresh chopped coriander
1 bunch green onions, washed and cut into strips
1 lb (500 g) fusilli

In a large saucepan melt 1 tsp (5 ml) of butter over medium heat. Add the onion, carrot and celery and cook 2 minutes.

Add the curry powder, lower the heat and cook slowly for 3 to 4 minutes to activate curry.

Add coconut milk and increase heat, reducing liquid by ⅓ and set aside.

In a second saucepan heat vegetable oil over high heat. Season shrimp with salt and pepper and quickly sear shrimp on both sides, about 10 to 15 seconds a side. Shrimp will curl and be about two-thirds cooked.

Boil fusilli until *al dente*. Drain and coat with remaining butter and keep warm.

Add shrimp, snow peas, coriander and green onions to sauce. Bring to a boil and season with salt and pepper to taste.

Add sauce to fusilli and toss. Serve immediately.

MAKES 4 SERVINGS.

GNOCCHI WITH HAZELNUT BUTTER

2 lb (1 kg) potatoes, peeled and quartered
2 large eggs, lightly beaten
1½ tsp (7 ml) salt
¼ tsp (1 ml) white pepper
¼ tsp (1 ml) nutmeg
2¼ cups (550 ml) all-purpose flour

BUTTER

½ cup (125 ml) butter
⅓ cup (75 ml) finely chopped hazelnuts
¼ tsp (1 ml) white pepper
Parmesan cheese to taste

In a saucepan boil potatoes in salted water until tender; drain and return potatoes to pan, drying over low heat about 3 minutes. Shake pan frequently. Remove from heat.

With an electric mixer whip potatoes until smooth; add eggs, salt, pepper and nutmeg blending until smooth.

Add 1½ cups (375 ml) flour, blending with a wooden spoon.

Knead in remaining flour a little at a time, on a floured board, until dough is no longer sticky.

Shape dough into ¾-inch (18-mm) ropes and cut each rope crosswise into ½-inch (12-mm) pieces.

Using a large saucepan, add gnocchi to boiling, salted water and cook until gnocchi float; remove with a slotted spoon to a colander and drain; keep warm.

In a saucepan melt butter, add hazelnuts and pepper; cook until hazelnuts are lightly browned.

Toss gnocchi with warm sauce.

Garnish with Parmesan cheese and serve immediately.

MAKES 8–10 SERVINGS.

Penne with Hazelnut and Sun-Dried Tomato Pesto

2 cups (500 ml) sun-dried tomatoes
3 garlic cloves
1¼ cups (300 ml) olive oil
½ cup (125 ml) chopped hazelnuts
½ cup (125 ml) Romano cheese
½ cup (125 ml) Parmesan cheese
1 lb (500 g) penne

In a food processor blend tomatoes, garlic, and oil until smooth.

Add hazelnuts and cheeses and process until blended (can be slightly chunky).

Boil penne until *al dente.* Drain and toss with pesto. Serve immediately.

MAKES 4 SERVINGS.

Fettucine with Macadamias

½ cup (125 ml) butter
2 cloves garlic, finely sliced
¼ cup (50 ml) thinly sliced onion
½ cup (125 ml) heavy cream
½ cup (125 ml) Parmesan cheese
1 lb (500 g) fettucine
4 oz (125 g) coarsely chopped macadamias
fresh ground pepper to taste
Parmesan cheese to taste

In a saucepan melt butter and sauté garlic and onion for 1 minute.

Stir in cream; remove from heat and stir in cheese.

Boil fettucine until *al dente.* Drain and toss with warm sauce and nuts.

Garnish with pepper and cheese and serve immediately.

MAKES 4 SERVINGS.

Vermicelli Caribbean Style

2 Tbsp (30 ml) olive oil
2 cloves garlic, chopped
2 boneless chicken breasts, cut into 1-inch (2.5-cm) pieces
1 tsp (5 ml) curry powder
1 tsp (5 ml) dried tarragon
1 Tbsp (15 ml) honey
1 tsp (5 ml) Dijon mustard
¼ cup (50 ml) orange juice
1 Tbsp (15 ml) marmalade

½ cup (125 ml) unsweetened coconut milk
½ cup (125 ml) chicken broth
¼ tsp (1 ml) salt
1 lb (500 g) vermicelli
½ cup (125 ml) chopped roasted unsalted peanuts

In a large skillet heat oil over medium heat and sauté garlic until soft. Add chicken and sauté until browned on all sides.

Reduce heat and add spices; continue to sauté another half minute.

Add honey, mustard, orange juice, marmalade, coconut milk and chicken broth. Bring to a boil, cover and simmer 15 minutes.

Increase heat to high, boiling uncovered for 5 minutes, until thick. Add salt.

Boil vermicelli until *al dente*. Drain and toss with warm sauce. Garnish with peanuts and serve immediately.

MAKES 4 SERVINGS.

REESE'S SPAGHETTI WITH PEANUT BUTTER

½ cup (125 ml) peanut butter
¼ cup (50 ml) chopped green onion
2 Tbsp (30 ml) soy sauce
1 garlic clove, minced
1 tsp (5 ml) finely chopped fresh ginger
2 tsp (10 ml) hot pepper sauce
⅔ cup (150 ml) chicken broth
2 Tbsp (30 ml) fresh lime juice
2 Tbsp (30 ml) peanut oil
2 lb (1 kg) cooked chicken, cut in 1-inch (2.5-cm) pieces
3 cups (750 ml) thin red bell pepper strips
1 lb (500 g) spaghetti

In a large saucepan stir together peanut butter, green onion, soy sauce, garlic, ginger and hot pepper sauce. Stir in broth until smooth.

Slowly add oil and lime juice, stirring until well blended. Cook until warm over medium heat. Do not boil.

Stir in chicken and peppers.

Boil spaghetti until *al dente.* Drain and toss with warm sauce. Serve immediately.

MAKES 4 SERVINGS.

RIGATONI WITH PINE NUTS

4 oz (125 g) pine nuts
⅓ cup (75 ml) sun-dried tomatoes
4 Tbsp (60 ml) olive oil
1 large onion, finely chopped
4 cloves garlic, finely chopped
2 Tbsp (30 ml) capers
salt, pepper to taste
1 lb (500 g) rigatoni
Parmesan cheese to taste

Toast pine nuts 5 minutes at 350° F (180° C).

Soften sun-dried tomatoes in 1½ cups (375 ml) boiling water for 5 minutes, covered; remove tomatoes and reserve 1 cup (250 ml) water.

Cut tomatoes into small pieces and set aside.

In a skillet sauté onion and garlic in oil; add liquid from tomatoes.

Stir in sun-dried tomatoes, capers and pine nuts; season with salt and pepper.

Boil rigatoni until *al dente.* Drain and toss with sauce.

Garnish with Parmesan cheese and serve immediately.

MAKES 4 SERVINGS.

ROTELLE WITH PESTO

2 cups (500 ml) fresh basil
½ cup (125 ml) olive oil
2 Tbsp (30 ml) pine nuts (or pistachios or walnuts)
2 cloves garlic
½ tsp (2 ml) salt
½ cup (125 ml) grated Parmesan cheese
2 Tbsp (30 ml) Romano cheese
3 Tbsp (45 ml) butter, softened
1 lb (500 g) rotelle
Parmesan cheese to taste
fresh ground pepper to taste

In a food processor or blender combine basil, oil, nuts, garlic and salt on high.

Place in a bowl and stir in cheeses; beat in butter.

Boil rotelle until *al dente*. Add several tablespoons of boiling water from the pasta to warm and thin pesto. Drain and toss rotelle with pesto sauce.

Garnish with Parmesan cheese and fresh ground pepper and serve immediately.

MAKES 4 SERVINGS.

LINGUINE WITH PINE NUTS, BACON AND SUN-DRIED TOMATOES

3 Tbsp (45 ml) pine nuts
1 Tbsp (15 ml) olive oil
4 bacon slices, chopped in ¼-inch (6-mm) pieces
2 large shallots, finely chopped
½ cup (125 ml) whipping cream
¼ cup (50 ml) oil-packed sun-dried tomatoes, drained and finely sliced
½ lb (250 g) linguine
¼ cup (50 ml) Romano or Parmesan cheese
fresh minced parsley to taste
Romano or Parmesan cheese to taste
fresh ground pepper to taste

Toast pine nuts in oven until brown.

In a frying pan heat oil over medium heat. Add bacon and cook until fat is rendered and bacon begins to color, about 6 minutes. Drain fat.

Add shallots and stir 2 minutes.

Add cream and just bring to a boil. Turn off frying pan and add sun-dried tomatoes.

Boil linguine until *al dente.* Drain and toss with ¼ cup (50 ml) of cheese and parsley, coating thoroughly.

Toss with sauce and pine nuts.

Garnish with Romano cheese and fresh ground papper and serve immediately.

MAKES 2 SERVINGS.

PENNE WITH WALNUTS AND ROQUEFORT SAUCE

1½ cups (375 ml) heavy cream
5 oz (140 g) Roquefort cheese, crumbled
6 Tbsp (90 ml) butter
black pepper
¾ cup (175 ml) coarsely chopped walnuts
1 lb (500 g) penne
¼ cup (50 ml) finely chopped parsley

In a saucepan simmer cream until reduced by half and whisk in cheese, butter and pepper; keep warm without boiling.

Toast walnuts on a baking sheet in oven until brown.

Boil penne until *al dente.* Drain and toss with warm sauce and walnuts.

Garnish with parsley and serve immediately.

MAKES 4 SERVINGS.

TAGLIATELLE WITH WALNUTS

4 Tbsp (60 ml) butter
1 clove garlic
1½ cups (375 ml) finely chopped walnuts
1 lb (500 g) pasta
¾ cup (175 ml) Parmesan cheese
7 oz (200 g) Mascarpone or cream cheese
pepper to taste

In a frying pan melt butter and sauté garlic; add nuts and stir 3 minutes. Remove from heat.
Boil pasta until *al dente*. Drain and toss with Parmesan cheese. Keep warm.
Add Mascarpone to nut mixture and heat gently; toss pasta with sauce.
Garnish with pepper and serve immediately.

MAKES 4 SERVINGS.

WALNUT SAUCE

1½ cups (375 ml) walnuts
¾ cup (175 ml) olive oil
4 Tbsp (60 ml) butter
½ cup (125 ml) Parmesan cheese
5 Tbsp (100 ml) heavy cream
salt

In a food processor or blender chop nuts; add olive oil and butter.
Add cheese, cream and salt and blend briefly.
Toss with pasta and serve hot.

MAKES 2 CUPS.

RICOTTA NUT SAUCE

½ cup (125 ml) chopped walnuts
½ cup (125 ml) pine nuts
1 cup (250 ml) ricotta
½ tsp (2 ml) sugar
1 Tbsp (15 ml) dried mint
2 Tbsp (30 ml) olive oil
1 clove garlic, finely chopped
2 large tomatoes, chopped
¼ cup (50 ml) dry white wine
1 tsp (5 ml) finely chopped fresh basil
salt, pepper to taste

Spread nuts on a baking sheet and toast 3 minutes at 325° F (160° C) until golden; do not overheat.
Place toasted nuts in a food processor or blender and blend until finely chopped.
In a bowl combine nuts, ricotta, sugar and mint. Set aside.

In a saucepan heat oil and sauté garlic; add tomatoes and cook 2 minutes.

Add wine and basil and simmer 10 minutes; add salt and pepper, then combine with nut mixture.

Heat through.

Toss with pasta and serve hot.

MAKES 2 CUPS.

Vegetables

ASPARAGUS ALMANDINE

24 asparagus spears
¼ cup (50 ml) butter
2 Tbsp (30 ml) Parmesan cheese
2 Tbsp (30 ml) blanched slivered almonds

Clean and trim asparagus and place in a shallow casserole dish.

Drizzle with butter and Parmesan cheese.

Bake 5 minutes at 400° F (200° C).

Sprinkle almonds on dish and continue baking 5 more minutes.

MAKES 6–8 SERVINGS.

ALMOND CELERY CASSEROLE

4 cups (1 L) celery, cut in ½-inch (1.2-cm) pieces
¾ cup (175 ml) blanched almonds, halved
2 Tbsp (30 ml) butter
2 Tbsp (30 ml) flour
1 10-oz (285-ml) can condensed cream of chicken soup
½ cup (125 ml) milk
1 egg, beaten
¾ cup (175 ml) dry bread crumbs
¼ cup (50 ml) melted butter

Steam or boil celery until almost tender and drain.

In a 2½-qt (3-L) casserole dish mix celery and almonds.

In a saucepan melt butter and blend in flour, soup and milk; cook until thickened.

Remove from heat and quickly stir in beaten egg.

Pour mixture over celery and blend thoroughly.

Drizzle bread crumbs with butter and bake 45 minutes at 300° F (150° C).

MAKES 8 SERVINGS.

ALMOND AND BROWN RICE PILAF

4 Tbsp (60 ml) butter, divided
½ cup (125 ml) slivered almonds
1 cup (250 ml) long grain brown rice, rinsed, drained and dried on paper towels
1 cup (250 ml) thinly sliced carrots
1 cup (250 ml) thinly sliced mushrooms
1 cup (250 ml) diced celery
1 10-oz (284-ml) can beef broth
1 Tbsp (15 ml) soy sauce
1 cup (250 ml) water
½ cup (125 ml) finely chopped scallions
1½ Tbsp (25 ml) chopped fresh parsley

In a skillet melt 2 Tbsp (30 ml) butter, add almonds and cook several minutes until golden brown; drain on paper towels and set aside.

Add remaining butter to skillet; add rice and cook several minutes, until browned.

Add carrots, mushrooms, celery, broth, soy sauce and water to rice and bring to a boil over high heat.

Reduce heat and simmer, covered for 25 minutes.

Place rice mixture in a greased, 9-inch (22-cm) baking dish.

Stir in onions and parsley and bake covered for 15 minutes at 350° F (180° C).

Stir in almonds and serve immediately.

MAKES 6 SERVINGS.

CASHEW BROCCOLI CASSEROLE

1½ cups (375 ml) uncooked brown rice
2 lbs (1 kg) broccoli, rinsed and trimmed
2 Tbsp (30 ml) vegetable oil
1 large onion, chopped
2 cloves garlic, minced
½ tsp (2 ml) dill
½ tsp (2 ml) thyme
1 tsp (5 ml) oregano
¼ cup (50 ml) fresh minced parsley
½ lb (250 g) mushrooms, sliced
1 green pepper, seeded and sliced
1½ cups (375 ml) cashews
½ lb (250 g) Swiss cheese
2 Tbsp (30 ml) Parmesan cheese

Cook rice according to package directions and set aside.

Cut broccoli into small florets.

In a large skillet heat oil over medium heat and add onion, garlic and spices, sautéing until onion is soft.

Stir in broccoli, mushrooms and green pepper, cooking until broccoli is tender.

Remove from heat and add cashews.

Spread rice in a greased 9-inch (22-cm) square pan.

Spoon on vegetable mixture and sprinkle with cheeses.

Bake 15 minutes at 350° F (180° C) until bubbly.

MAKES 8 SERVINGS.

STEWED CHESTNUTS

1 lb (500 g) chestnuts (about 2½ cups (625 ml) unshelled)
water
2 cups (500 ml) chicken stock
butter to taste
salt, pepper to taste

Wash chestnuts, discarding any that float.

Cut a slit or an X into the shell of each chestnut, place in a pot and barely cover with water; boil 15 to 20 minutes.

Remove shells and inner skins while still hot.

Stew chestnuts in water or chicken stock for 15 minutes or until tender.

Drain well and serve hot with butter, salt and pepper.

MAKES 4 SERVINGS.

CHESTNUTS AND BRUSSELS SPROUTS

1 lb (500 g) chestnuts
½ cup (125 ml) butter
1 lb (500 g) Brussels sprouts
salt, pepper to taste

Prepare chestnuts as in Stewed Chestnuts (see above); however, instead of stewing, fry for 5 minutes in melted butter.

Remove outer leaves from Brussels sprouts and cut a cross in the bases.

Cook in boiling water or steam until tender.

Drain and toss with chestnuts.

Serve hot with salt and pepper to taste.

MAKES 6–8 SERVINGS.

CHESTNUTS AND SWEET POTATOES

6 medium sweet potatoes
1 lb (500 g) chestnuts
2 tsp (10 ml) butter
½ cup (125 ml) brown sugar
¼ cup (50 ml) water
¼ cup (50 ml) butter
½ tsp (2 ml) cinnamon
¼ tsp (1 ml) nutmeg
½ cup (125 ml) buttered dry bread crumbs

Wash, pare and slice sweet potatoes; boil 5 minutes and drain.

Prepare Stewed Chestnuts (see previous page).

Grease a 9 x 13-inch (22 x 33-cm) casserole with 2 tsp (10 ml) of butter and layer the sweet potatoes and chestnuts alternately.

In a saucepan boil remaining ingredients except bread crumbs.

Pour sauce over layered vegetables. Cover with bread crumbs and bake 15–20 minutes, until potatoes are tender, at 350° F (180° C).

MAKES 6 SERVINGS.

CHESTNUT PURÉE

3 cups (750 ml) roasted chestnuts (see page 30)
4 cups (1 L) chicken broth
salt, pepper to taste
2 cups (500 ml) cream

Remove shells and skins from roasted chestnuts while still hot; add to broth and simmer until soft.

Strain chestnuts, reserving liquid. Purée chestnuts in blender or food processor and return to broth and simmer until thick.

Add salt, pepper and cream.

Use for soups, soufflés and stuffings, or serve as a condiment with game.

MAKES ABOUT 6 CUPS (1.5 L).

CHESTNUT POTATO PURÉE

1¾ cups (425 ml) potatoes, peeled and cut in large pieces
½ cup (125 ml) butter
1½ lbs (750 g) fresh or canned chestnut purée
⅓ cup (75 ml) sour cream
1 egg
1 egg yolk

4 Tbsp (60 ml) Calvados
1 tsp (5 ml) cardamon
1½ tsp (7 ml) salt
pinch cayenne pepper
¼ cup (50 ml) butter

Cook potatoes in salted water until tender; drain well.

Mash potatoes with butter and combine with chestnut purée.

Whisk in remaining ingredients except for remaining butter.

Butter a 1½-qt (2-L) soufflé dish with half the remaining butter.

Spoon purée into dish and dot with remaining butter.

Bake 25 minutes at 350° F (180° C).

MAKES 6 SERVINGS.

SPINACH, MUSHROOM AND CHESTNUT CASSEROLE

3 10-oz (300-g) packages frozen spinach
½ lb (250 g) sliced mushrooms
1½ Tbsp (25 ml) lemon juice
3 Tbsp (45 ml) butter
2 Tbsp (30 ml) butter
1½ Tbsp (25 ml) flour
1 cup (250 ml) milk
2 egg yolks, beaten
½ cup (125 ml) grated Swiss cheese
½ cup (125 ml) dry bread crumbs
6½ oz (185 g) peeled chestnuts

Cook spinach according to package directions; press out water until nearly dry.

Sprinkle mushrooms with lemon juice and cook in 3 Tbsp (45 ml) butter over moderate heat 5 minutes; mix with spinach.

Arrange spinach in a shallow buttered 2-qt (2.5-L) casserole dish.

In a saucepan make a white sauce by melting 2 Tbsp (30 ml) butter and stirring in flour over low heat until blended; gradually add milk stirring continuously until thick. Add egg yolks; stir until blended.

Boil chestnuts until tender, add to white sauce and pour over spinach mixture.

Combine grated cheese and bread crumbs and sprinkle over the top.

Bake 30–35 minutes at 350° F (180° C).

MAKES 6–8 SERVINGS.

STUFFED ACORN SQUASH

2 medium-sized acorn squash
1 lb (500 g) chestnuts
¼ cup (50 ml) raisins
¼ cup (50 ml) black walnut pieces
2 carrots, finely chopped
2 Tbsp (30 ml) butter
4 Tbsp (60 ml) maple syrup
¼ cup (50 ml) butter

Slice squash in half lengthwise, scoop out and discard seedy pulp and place square halves in deep baking dish, open side up.

Roast, peel and chop chestnuts; mix together with carrots, raisins and walnut pieces.

Fill squash cavities with mixture.

Dot with butter, cover and bake 1 hour at 375° F (190° C).

Melt butter with maple syrup and drizzle over tops before serving.

MAKES 4 SERVINGS.

NEW POTATOES AND GREEN BEANS IN HOT COCONUT CREAM

¾ cup (175 ml) heavy cream
¾ cup (175 ml) whole milk
¾ cup (175 ml) unsweetened dried coconut
3 cloves garlic, chopped
2 lbs (1 kg) new potatoes
1¼ lbs (625 g) green beans
hot peppers, to taste (optional)
3 Tbsp (45 ml) butter
2 tsp (10 ml) peeled grated fresh ginger
2 tsp (10 ml) cumin
½ tsp (2 ml) coriander seed
½ cup (125 ml) water
salt to taste

In a heavy saucepan combine cream, milk, coconut and garlic and simmer about 30 minutes; set aside.

Wash potatoes and cut into large pieces.

Rinse beans, trim and cut in half.

Dice peppers and set aside.

In a large pan melt butter and add spices, cooking 4 minutes; add potatoes and stir until coated with butter mixture.

Pour in water, cover pan and cook 10 minutes; uncover pan, add beans, and cook until water has evaporated and vegetables are almost tender.

Strain coconut-cream mixture, pressing coconut to release as much liquid as possible; add liquid to vegetables.

Increase heat to cook vegetables and reduce cream to a sauce.

Stir in peppers and cook 2 more minutes. Serve hot.

MAKES 6 SERVINGS.

HAZELNUT SCALLOPED POTATOES

¾ cup (175 ml) chopped toasted hazelnuts, skins removed
3 large potatoes, sliced
1 cup (250 ml) grated Cheddar cheese
2 Tbsp (30 ml) finely chopped onions
2 Tbsp (30 ml) butter
half a 10-oz can (284-ml) condensed cream of mushroom soup
¾ cup (175 ml) milk
1 tsp (5 ml) salt
⅛ tsp (.5 ml) pepper

Arrange four layers: nuts, potatoes, cheese and onions in a 4-cup (1-L) casserole dish.

Dot top with butter.

Combine soup, milk, salt and pepper and pour over layers.

Bake 50 minutes at 350° F (180° C), until potatoes are tender.

MAKES 6 SERVINGS.

PEANUT RICE CASSEROLE

3½ cups (875 ml) cooked rice
1 cup (250 ml) peanut butter
2 cups (500 ml) milk
2 tsp (10 ml) chives
2 tsp (10 ml) chili powder
¼ tsp (1 ml) ginger
½ tsp (2 ml) salt
2 cloves garlic, minced
1 cup (250 ml) shredded cheddar cheese
3 Tbsp (45 ml) chopped pimento

In a buttered 2-qt (2.5-L) casserole place half the rice.

In a bowl combine peanut butter and milk and add spices and garlic.

In a separate bowl combine cheese and pimento.

Pour half the peanut mixture over rice and top with half the cheese mixture.

Top with remaining rice, then remaining peanut mixture.

Bake 35–40 minutes at 375° F (190° C).

Remove from oven and top with remaining cheese mixture; let stand 10 minutes until cheese melts, or return to oven for 5 minutes.

MAKES 6–8 SERVINGS.

PECAN APPLE SQUASH

2 acorn squash
½ cup (125 ml) butter
2 cups (500 ml) finely chopped apples
1½ tsp (7 ml) cinnamon
½ tsp (2 ml) salt
2 tsp (10 ml) lemon juice
1 cup (250 ml) chopped pecans
nutmeg to taste

Slice squash in half crosswise and remove seeds.

Bake cut side down in a shallow pan for 45 minutes at 350° F (180° C).

Remove cooked squash from shells and combine with remaining ingredients, reserving nutmeg and ¼ cup (50 ml) of chopped pecans.

Spoon mixture back into shells and top with pecans and nutmeg.

Bake 10 minutes at 350° F (180° C).

MAKES 4 SERVINGS.

CASSEROLE POTATOES AU GRATIN

4 cups (1 L) sliced potatoes
2 Tbsp (30 ml) butter
2 Tbsp (30 ml) flour
2 cups (500 ml) milk
1 tsp (5 ml) salt
¼ cup (50 ml) cheese
¼ cup (50 ml) grated pecans
2 Tbsp (30 ml) chopped onion
dry bread crumbs

Peel and slice potatoes very thinly.

In a saucepan make a white sauce by melting butter and stirring in flour until blended; gradually add milk stirring continuously until thick; add salt.

Place potatoes in a buttered casserole, alternating layers of pecans and cheese.

Sprinkle with chopped onion.

Pour sauce over layers and sprinkle with bread crumbs.

Bake 45 minutes at 350° F (180° C).

MAKES 4–6 SERVINGS.

PECAN SWEET POTATO CAKES

6 Tbsp (90 ml) butter
6 Tbsp (90 ml) chopped toasted pecans
6 cups (1.5 L) sweet potatoes, peeled and shredded
salt, cinnamon to taste
sour cream to garnish

Using a non-stick skillet, melt butter over medium heat.

Add 1 Tbsp (15 ml) of chopped pecans and place 1 cup (250 ml) of shredded sweet potatoes over butter and pecans.

Sprinkle lightly with salt.

Brown quickly, watching carefully for burning. Turn and form a round pancake.

Brown second side and transfer to a greased baking sheet.

Repeat procedure, making 6 potato patties.

Bake 10 minutes at 350° F (180° C).

Sprinkle with cinnamon and serve hot with sour cream.

MAKES 6 PATTIES.

PECAN AND SWEET POTATO CASSEROLE

6 large sweet potatoes, peeled, cooked and whipped until fluffy
2 Tbsp (30 ml) softened butter
juice of 2 oranges
grated zest of 2 oranges
4 eggs
2 Tbsp (30 ml) butter
¾ cup (175 ml) sugar
1 cup (250 ml) firmly packed brown sugar
2 Tbsp (30 ml) all-purpose flour
1 cup (250 ml) chopped pecans

In a 3-quart (4-L) casserole place sweet potatoes and add butter, juice, orange zest, eggs and sugar and beat well. Bake 30 minutes at 350° F (180° C).

In a saucepan combine butter, sugars and flour and cook on low heat until sugars dissolve, stirring constantly.

Pour sauce over sweet potato mixture and top with pecans. Serve immediately.

MAKES 8–10 SERVINGS.

PINE NUT CARROT STIR FRY

2 Tbsp (30 ml) butter
1 Tbsp (15 ml) vegetable oil
2 cups (500 ml) julienned carrots
¼ cup (50 ml) water
1 cup (250 ml) julienned zucchini
¾ cup (175 ml) sliced mushrooms
4 green onions, chopped
½ tsp (2 ml) ginger
¼ tsp (1 ml) salt
⅛ tsp (.5 ml) pepper
½ cup (125 ml) pine nuts

In a skillet heat 1 Tbsp (15 ml) butter and oil and stir-fry carrots for 2 minutes.

Add water, cover and simmer 3 minutes; remove lid.

Add remaining butter, vegetables and seasonings and stir-fry 5 minutes.

Toss in pine nuts and serve immediately.

MAKES 4–6 SERVINGS.

SWISS CHARD AND PINE NUTS

2 Tbsp (30 ml) olive oil
1 clove garlic, minced
¼ cup (50 ml) pine nuts
3–4 large Swiss chard leaves
pinch sugar
2 Tbsp (30 ml) Parmesan cheese
pinch salt
fresh ground pepper to taste

In a non-aluminum skillet heat oil and sauté garlic and pine nuts over low heat until nuts are golden, about 5 minutes.

Trim thick stems from chard and coarsely shred to yield 3 cups (750 ml).

Place chard in skillet and sauté over medium heat 5 to 10 minutes until limp and tender.

Discard garlic.

Sprinkle chard with sugar and cheese. Toss to coat and season with salt and pepper and serve immediately.

MAKES 2 SERVINGS.

WALNUT CARROT SOUFFLÉ

3 cups (750 ml) sliced carrots
2 eggs, separated
½ cup (125 ml) sour cream
2 Tbsp (30 ml) butter
2 Tbsp (30 ml) honey
¼ tsp (1 ml) salt
¼ tsp (1 ml) nutmeg
½ cup (125 ml) chopped walnuts

- Cook carrots until tender; drain, mash and purée in a blender or food processor.
- Beat in remaining ingredients, except for egg whites, until well blended.
- Beat egg whites until stiff and carefully fold into carrot mixture.
- Pour into a greased 4-cup (1-L) casserole dish.
- Bake 40 minutes at 350° F (180° C).
- Serve immediately.

MAKES 4 SERVINGS.

ALMOND AND WILD RICE STUFFING

3 oz (85 g) wild rice
2½ cups (625 ml) chicken stock or bouillon
2 Tbsp (30 ml) butter
⅔ cup (150 ml) chopped celery
⅔ cup (150 ml) chopped onion
½ cup (125 ml) cooked white rice
½ cup (125 ml) walnuts
⅛ tsp (.5 ml) sage
⅓ cup (75 ml) sherry

- In a saucepan cook rice in chicken stock until tender, about 30 minutes.
- Drain and reserve liquid.
- In a skillet melt butter and sauté celery and onion until tender.
- In a mixing bowl combine all ingredients using chicken stock to add desired moistness.
- Best served with cornish hens.

MAKES ABOUT 5 CUPS (1 L 250 ML).

ALMOND STUFFING

2 cups (500 ml) minced onion
1 lb (500 g) melted butter
2 cups (500 ml) chopped celery
1 tsp (5 ml) thyme
1 tsp (5 ml) marjoram
1 tsp (5 ml) savory
1 tsp (5 ml) sage
10 cups (2.5 L) soft bread crumbs
2½ cups (625 ml) toasted slivered almonds

- Sauté onion in a ¼ lb (125 g) of butter.
- In a mixing bowl combine all ingredients.
- Best served with turkey.

MAKES 16 CUPS (4 L).

HAZELNUT STUFFING

¼ cup (50 ml) butter
¼ cup (50 ml) finely chopped onion
¼ cup (50 ml) celery, diced
¼ cup (50 ml) chopped mushrooms
1 tsp (5 ml) salt
½ tsp (2 ml) thyme
¼ tsp (1 ml) poultry seasoning
pinch cayenne pepper
pinch garlic powder
2 cups (500 ml) soft bread crumbs
½ cup (125 ml) chicken broth
¾ cup (175 ml) finely chopped hazelnuts

In a skillet melt butter and sauté onion, celery, mushrooms and seasonings.

Add bread crumbs, broth and nuts and mix lightly.

Best served with turkey breast, veal or lamb.

MAKES 2½ CUPS (625 ML).

CHESTNUT STUFFING

½ lb (250 g) chestnuts
¼ cup (50 ml) melted butter
2 cups (500 ml) soft bread crumbs
1 tsp (5 ml) salt
2 tsp (10 ml) poultry seasoning
1 egg, well beaten
¼ cup (50 ml) diced celery

Roast or stew chestnuts (see page 121) and chop finely.

In a mixing bowl combine chestnuts with remaining ingredients.

Best served with fowl.

MAKES 3 CUPS (750 ML).

CHESTNUT AND OYSTER STUFFING

½ cup (125 ml) butter
6 cups (1.5 L) bread cubes
1 medium onion, chopped
2 cups (500 ml) diced celery
2 cups (500 ml) cooked, drained and chopped chestnuts
8–10 medium oysters, chopped
1 shredded wheat biscuit, crushed
1½ tsp (7 ml) Worcestershire sauce
1 clove garlic, minced
1 tsp (5 ml) salt
½ tsp (2 ml) poultry seasoning
¼ tsp (1 ml) thyme
¼ tsp (1 ml) rosemary
⅛ tsp (.5 ml) pepper
½ cup (125 ml) melted butter

- Melt butter in a skillet and sauté bread cubes until browned.
- In a mixing bowl combine all ingredients well.
- Best served with turkey.

MAKES 11 CUPS (3.75 L).

PEANUT STUFFING

1½ cups (375 ml) cracker crumbs
1 cup (500 ml) peanuts
1 cup (500 ml) heavy cream
4 Tbsp (60 ml) butter
1 tsp (5 ml) minced onion
salt, pepper, cayenne pepper to taste

- In a blender or food processor, process cracker crumbs and peanuts.
- Add remaining ingredients and blend with a fork.
- Best served with duck.

MAKES 3 CUPS (750 ML).

PINE NUT AND SAUSAGE STUFFING

1 cup (250 ml) whipping cream
3 cups (750 ml) soft bread crumbs
1 lb (500 g) sweet Italian sausage
½ cup (125 ml) butter
1 lb (500 g) cooked ham, diced
1 cup (250 ml) sliced fresh mushrooms
¼ cup (50 ml) chopped parsley
½ tsp (2 ml) basil
½ tsp (2 ml) tarragon
¼ tsp (1 ml) nutmeg
1 tsp (5 ml) ginger
¼ cup (50 ml) chopped pine nuts
¼ cup (50 ml) chopped walnuts
½ cup (125 ml) Parmesan cheese

- In a large bowl pour cream over bread crumbs and set aside.
- Remove sausage from casing and brown in a skillet; add butter, ham, mushrooms and spices.
- Cook for 10 minutes and remove from heat.
- When cool add nuts, cheese and bread-crumb mixture, blending throughly.
- Best served with fowl.

MAKES 7 CUPS (2.25 L).

RICE STUFFING WITH ALMONDS AND PISTACHIOS

3½ cups (875 ml) chicken broth
¼ tsp (1 ml) saffron threads (optional)
¼ cup (50 ml) oil
1 cup (250 ml) minced onions
1¾ cups (425 ml) long-grain rice
¼ tsp (1 ml) salt
pepper to taste
½ cup (125 ml) raisins
½ cup (125 ml) slivered toasted almonds
½ cup (125 ml) toasted pistachios

In a medium saucepan boil broth and add saffron; cover and keep warm.

In a skillet heat oil and sauté onions until soft; add rice and stir 4 minutes or until grains turn milky.

Bring broth to a boil and pour over rice; stir and add salt and pepper.

Bring to a boil and transfer to oven for 10 minutes at 400° F (200° C).

Stir in raisins and continue to bake 10 minutes longer until rice is tender.

Fold in nuts.

Best served with turkey or chicken.

MAKES 8 CUPS (2 L).

WALNUT STUFFING

giblets from fowl
1 onion, chopped
1 bay leaf
1 cup (250 ml) boiling water
6 cups (1.5 L) soft bread crumbs
1 Tbsp (15 ml) salt
2 Tbsp (30 ml) poultry seasoning
2 cups (500 ml) chopped walnuts
4 Tbsp (60 ml) cooking oil

In a saucepan cook giblets, onion and bay leaf several minutes in boiling water until tender.

Remove giblets with a slotted spoon and chop finely.

Add remaining ingredients to giblets and toss lightly; moisten with giblet stock.

Best served with turkey or chicken.

MAKES 8 CUPS (2 L).

Main Courses: Chicken, Meat, and Seafood

Main Courses: Chicken, Meat & Seafood

Chicken Main Dishes

Almond Chicken Thighs

8 chicken thighs, deboned
salt
2 Tbsp (30 ml) minced onion
16 dried apricot halves
½ cup (125 ml) toasted slivered almonds

Sauce

½ cup (125 ml) sour cream
6 Tbsp (90 ml) apricot jam
1 Tbsp (15 ml) prepared mustard

- Place thighs skin side down and sprinkle chicken with salt and onion.
- Place 2 apricot halves and 1 Tbsp (15 ml) of almonds in center of each thigh and fold sides over, fastening with toothpicks.
- Place rolls skin side down on baking sheet and bake 40 minutes at 400° F (200° C).
- In a saucepan combine sauce ingredients and heat; do not boil.
- Serve over chicken.

Makes 4 servings.

Chicken Almandine

2 Tbsp (30 ml) butter
1 cup (250 ml) uncooked rice
2 cups (500 ml) sliced mushrooms
½ cup (125 ml) blanched slivered almonds
1 onion, finely chopped
½ green pepper, finely chopped
2 cups (500 ml) hot water
½ tsp (2 ml) salt
2 cups (500 ml) chopped cooked chicken
1 10-oz (285-ml) can condensed mushroom soup
8 oz (250 ml) sour cream
parsley
toasted almonds

In a frying pan melt butter and stir in rice, mushrooms, slivered almonds, onion and green pepper; cook until lightly brown, stirring frequently.

Stir in water and salt and bring to a boil.

Cover and reduce heat, simmering 15 minutes; stir occasionally.

When rice is tender add cooked chicken, mushroom soup and sour cream; blend thoroughly, but do not boil.

Transfer to a casserole dish for serving and keep warm in the oven.

Garnish with parsley and toasted almonds.

MAKES 6–8 SERVINGS.

CHICKEN AND CASHEWS

SAUCE

2 Tbsp (30 ml) bean sauce (sold in Oriental groceries)
2 Tbsp (30 ml) soy sauce
2 tsp (10 ml) sugar
1 tsp (5 ml) vinegar

CHICKEN

1 egg white
1 Tbsp (15 ml) cornstarch
1/8 tsp (.5 ml) salt
1 lb (500 g) chicken, skinned, deboned and cut into bite-size pieces
peanut oil

VEGETABLES

1 medium bell pepper, seeded and diced
8-oz (250-ml) can bamboo shoots, drained
2 tsp (10 ml) garlic, finely chopped
1/4 cup (50 ml) cashews
2 Tbsp (30 ml) rice wine

Stir together ingredients for sauce and set aside.

In a medium bowl combine egg white, corn starch and salt, and coat chicken well.

In a heavy skillet or wok heat about 3 inches (8 cm) of oil until a haze forms.

Fry chicken until golden brown and remove with a slotted spoon; drain on paper towels and keep warm. Discard oil.

Clean skillet and add 2 Tbsp (30 ml) of fresh oil.

Sauté vegetables and garlic until crisp-tender.

Add chicken and cashews and sprinkle with rice wine.

Stir in sauce, heat and serve immediately.

Best served with rice.

MAKES 4 SERVINGS.

CHICKEN CASHEW CASSEROLE

2 cups (500 ml) diced cooked chicken
1 10-oz (285-ml) can condensed mushroom soup
½ cup (125 ml) cashew nuts, whole or pieces
¼ cup (50 ml) finely chopped onion
¼ cup (50 ml) diced celery
1 tsp (5 ml) salt
¼ tsp (1 ml) pepper
whole cashew nuts

In a mixing bowl combine all ingredients except whole cashews and place in a lightly buttered 2-qt (2.5-L) casserole dish.

Cover and bake 30 minutes at 350° F (180° C).

Garnish with whole cashews.

MAKES 6–8 SERVINGS.

WARM CHICKEN SALAD

4 chicken breasts, skinned, deboned and cut into bite-size pieces
¼ cup (50 ml) cornstarch
¼ cup (50 ml) cooking oil
2 garlic buds, minced
1 cup (250 ml) sliced fresh mushrooms
1 cup (250 ml) green onions cut in large pieces
1 cup (250 ml) celery, sliced on the diagonal
¼ cup (50 ml) soy sauce
1 large tomato, cut in chunks
2 cups (500 ml) shredded lettuce
½ cup (125 ml) whole cashews

Coat chicken pieces in cornstarch and brown quickly in cooking oil.

Add garlic and vegetables and sauté for 1 minute.

Stir in soy sauce, cover and simmer 5 minutes.

Add tomato chunks, lettuce and cashews, cover and let stand 1 minute.

Serve immediately.

MAKES 4 SERVINGS.

MAR HI GAI (CHINESE CHESTNUT CHICKEN)

1 clove garlic
1 Tbsp (15 ml) vegetable oil
4 thick slices peeled raw ginger
2 chicken breasts, skinned, deboned and chopped in pieces
2 Tbsp (30 ml) sherry
1 tsp (5 ml) honey
pepper to taste
soy sauce to taste
½ lb (250 g) chestnuts
½ cup (125 ml) hot water
4 cups (1 L) cooked rice

In a large skillet or wok sauté minced garlic in oil until soft.

Add ginger and stir; add chicken pieces and brown all sides.

Stir in sherry, honey, pepper and soy sauce; cover and simmer 20 minutes.

Cut chestnuts in half (from top to bottom) and boil in water for 5 minutes.

Drain, peel and chop chestnuts into large pieces.

Add chestnuts to chicken and simmer several more minutes until liquid is reduced.

Remove ginger pieces and serve over rice.

MAKES 4 SERVINGS.

CURRIED COCONUT CHICKEN

2 lb (1 kg) chicken, skinned, deboned and cut into strips
½ cup (125 ml) curry powder
¼ cup (50 ml) clarified butter
1 ripe papaya, peeled, seeded and diced
2 bananas, sliced diagonally
4 Tbsp (60 ml) toasted coconut flakes
6 Tbsp (90 ml) cream of coconut
½ tsp (2 ml) salt
½ tsp (2 ml) white pepper
½ cup (125 ml) dark rum

Dredge chicken in curry.

In a skillet heat butter and cook chicken until dark brown.

Add remaining ingredients and stir quickly.

Let rum burn off and serve immediately.

MAKES 4 SERVINGS.

PECAN-CRUSTED CHICKEN

1 cup (250 ml) all-purpose flour
1 tsp (5 ml) salt
½ tsp (2 ml) pepper
2 egg whites, beaten
6 Tbsp (90 ml) Dijon mustard
1 cup (250 ml) finely ground pecans
1 cup (250 ml) dry bread crumbs
4 chicken breasts, skinned and deboned
4 Tbsp (60 ml) vegetable oil
½ cup (125 ml) heavy cream

Combine flour, salt and pepper and set aside.

Blend egg whites with 4 Tbsp (60 ml) mustard and set aside.

Combine pecans and bread crumbs.

Dredge each piece of chicken in flour, dip in egg white mixture, then pecan mixture.

Heat oil in skillet and brown chicken until crisp, about 3 minutes, on first side; turn and cook until done, about 5 minutes.

In a saucepan heat cream, adding remaining mustard; cook until hot, about 3 minutes.

Pour sauce over chicken and serve.

MAKES 4 SERVINGS.

PINE NUT CHICKEN

1 Tbsp (15 ml) butter
1 Tbsp (15 ml) finely chopped onion
½ cup (125 ml) diced celery
10 oz (300 g) frozen French-style green beans
2 cups (500 ml) diced cooked chicken
1 10-oz can (284-ml) condensed cream of mushroom soup
½ tsp (2 ml) oregano
⅛ tsp (.5 ml) white pepper
¾ cup (175 ml) pine nuts
1 Tbsp (15 ml) parsley

In a large saucepan melt butter and add onion, celery and beans.

Cover and simmer over low heat about 15 minutes, stirring occasionally until beans are tender.

Add chicken, soup and spices and cook 10 more minutes.

Stir in nuts and sprinkle with parsley. Serve immediately.

MAKES 4–6 SERVINGS.

BASQUE CHICKEN

Salad greens for four servings

Arrange salad greens on four plates and refrigerate until use.

CRUST

2 cups (500 ml) dry bread crumbs
⅔ cup (150 ml) pine nuts
2 Tbsp (30 ml) chopped garlic in oil
½ cup (125 ml) coarsely chopped cilantro
⅓ cup (75 ml) plus 1 Tbsp (15 ml) coarsely chopped parsley
⅓ cup (75 ml) plus 1 Tbsp (15 ml) melted butter

In a food processor combine all ingredients until well blended.

4 6-oz (170-g) chicken breasts, skinned and deboned
flour
2 eggs
1 cup (250 ml) milk
¼ cup (50 ml) melted butter

Pat chicken breasts with paper towels to dry, then dredge in flour to lightly coat, shaking off any excess flour.

In a bowl beat eggs and milk.

Dip chicken breasts in egg wash.

Press both sides of the chicken breasts into the nut mixture to form a crust.

Place coated chicken breasts into a baking dish and drizzle with melted butter.

Bake 15 to 20 minutes at 350°F (180° C), until chicken is cooked through.

VINAIGRETTE DRESSING

½ tsp (2 ml) salt
½ tsp (2 ml) pepper
½ cup (125 ml) plus 2 tsp (10 ml) olive oil
¼ cup (50 ml) lemon juice
½ tsp (2 ml) dry mustard
⅓ cup (75 ml) pine nuts
¼ cup (50 ml) plus 2 tsp (10 ml) finely chopped basil
¼ cup (50 ml) plus 2 tsp (10 ml) finely chopped oregano
⅓ cup (75 ml) plus 1 Tbsp (15 ml) finely chopped red bell pepper

In a bowl whisk salt, pepper, olive oil, lemon juice and dry mustard until well blended.

Place in a saucepan and add pine nuts, herbs and red bell pepper.

Bring dressing to a boil.

To serve, place warm chicken on salad greens and drizzle with hot dressing.

MAKES 4 SERVINGS.

CHICKEN AND WALNUTS

1 tsp (5 ml) salt
1 tsp (5 ml) sugar
½ tsp (2 ml) ginger
3 Tbsp (45 ml) soy sauce
2 cloves garlic, minced
2 large chicken breasts, skinned and deboned, cut into bite-size pieces
3 Tbsp (45 ml) peanut oil
1 cup (250 ml) walnuts
1 8-oz (250-g) can bamboo shoots, drained
1 Tbsp (15 ml) cornstarch
1 cup (250 ml) water

In a bowl combine salt, sugar, ginger, soy sauce and garlic and marinate chicken 20 minutes stirring occasionally.

In a heavy skillet heat oil and stir-fry walnuts 1 minute.

Remove walnuts with a slotted spoon and add chicken to oil. Cook 5 minutes, stirring constantly.

Mix in bamboo shoots.

Blend cornstarch and water and add to chicken, cooking until sauce is clear and thick.

Stir in walnuts and serve immediately.

MAKES 4 SERVINGS.

Meat Main Dishes

VEAL AND CASHEW STEW

½ cup (125 ml) flour
1½ lbs (750 g) veal, cut in cubes
¾ cup (175 ml) butter
1 onion, chopped
3 garlic cloves, minced
salt, pepper to taste
¼ tsp (1 ml) nutmeg
1 cup (250 ml) chicken stock
1 cup (250 ml) beef broth
1 lb (500 g) mushrooms, sliced
1½ cups (375 ml) cashews
3 Tbsp (45 ml) brandy
cashews

Place flour and veal in a bag and shake to coat veal.

In a Dutch oven brown veal in ½ cup (125 ml) butter; add onion and sauté until soft.

Stir in garlic, spices, chicken and beef stock; cover and bake 1 hour at 325° F (160° C).

Sauté mushrooms in remaining butter; add nuts and brandy.

Spoon sauce over veal and continue to bake another 15 minutes, until meat is tender.

Garnish with additional cashews.

MAKES 4 SERVINGS.

CHESTNUT TENDERLOIN WITH FRUIT MINGLE

4 Granny Smith apples, peeled and sliced in ¼-inch (6-mm) wedges
½ lb (250 g) dried chestnuts, rehydrated to 1 lb (.5 kg), or fresh chestnuts
15 dried or fresh black cherries, sliced in half
1 tsp (5 ml) sugar
1 cup (250 g) red wine
4 6-oz (170-g) beef tenderloin (or venison), ½-inch (12-mm) thick
2 Tbsp (30 ml) olive oil
sprigs of mint
salt, pepper to taste

In a shallow bowl place apples, chestnuts and cherries; sprinkle with sugar and wine and set aside half an hour.

In a skillet brown meat in olive oil; cook 4 minutes and set aside.

Pour chestnut mixture into skillet with meat juices; simmer 20 minutes.

Add meat and heat through.

Serve on a bed of mint.

MAKES 4 SERVINGS.

CHESTNUT STROGANOFF

1½ lbs (750 g) lean beef, cut in thin strips
1 Tbsp (15 ml) cooking oil
2 Tbsp (30 ml) butter
2 Tbsp (30 ml) all-purpose flour
pinch salt
½ tsp (2 ml) celery salt
½ tsp (2 ml) paprika
1¼ cups (300 ml) beef stock
½ cup (125 ml) sour cream
2 Tbsp (30 ml) cooking sherry
1 cup (250 ml) cooked chestnuts, mashed (see page 121)

In a frying pan brown beef in oil in batches; drain off excess fat. Set beef aside.

In a saucepan melt butter and blend in flour and seasonings.

Add beef stock and cook until smooth, stirring constantly.

Remove from heat and add sour cream and sherry; stir in chestnuts and blend well.

Add chestnut mixture to beef, heating until mixture bubbles and beef is cooked.

Serve over rice or noodles.

MAKES 4–6 SERVINGS.

CHESTNUT LOAF

1½ cups (375 ml) ground raw chestnuts
2 cups (500 ml) whole wheat dry bread crumbs
1½ cups (375 ml) finely chopped celery
1 cup (250 ml) finely ground carrots
1 garlic clove, minced
3 eggs, well beaten
½ cup (125 ml) cream
3 Tbsp (45 ml) minced parsley

Peel raw chestnuts and grind them in a food processor.
In a mixing bowl combine all ingredients.
Place in a greased 9 x 5 x 3-inch (23 x 13-cm) loaf pan.
Bake 45 minutes at 350° F (180° C).

MAKES 4 SERVINGS.

COCONUT MEATBALLS

¾ lb (375 g) lean ground beef
pinch salt
¼ tsp (1 ml) pepper
2 Tbsp (30 ml) flour
1 egg, beaten
1⅓ cups (325 ml) flaked coconut
pinch salt
cooking oil

SAUCE

¼ cup (50 ml) jelly (raspberry, black currant)
1 tsp (5 ml) dry mustard
1 tsp (5 ml) cider vinegar
¼ cup (50 ml) tomato chutney

In a mixing bowl combine beef, salt and pepper and shape into bite-size balls.
In a separate bowl add flour to beaten egg and combine well.
Mix coconut and a pinch of salt and place on a sheet of wax paper.
Roll meatballs in egg mixture, then coconut.
In a skillet brown meatballs in oil.
Place meatballs in a buttered casserole dish and bake 15 minutes at 350° F (180° C) until tender.
To make sauce, combine ingredients and heat in a saucepan.
Serve over meatballs.

MAKES 4 SERVINGS.

PORK AND BROCCOLI STIR-FRY IN PEANUT SAUCE

1 tsp (5 ml) sesame oil
1 clove garlic, chopped
1 large onion, chopped
¾ lb (375 g) lean pork, cut in 1-inch (2.5-cm) strips
¼ cup (50 ml) chunky peanut butter
3 Tbsp (45 ml) soy sauce
2 Tbsp (30 ml) orange juice
3 drops hot pepper sauce
1 bunch broccoli, stalk and florets trimmed in 1-inch (2.5-cm) pieces and blanched
¼ cup (50 ml) unsalted peanuts

In a wok heat oil and sauté garlic and onion; add pork and sauté about 5 minutes until browned on all sides.

In a mixing bowl combine peanut butter, soy sauce, orange juice and hot pepper sauce. Add to pork and cook another 5 minutes.

Push pork to outer edges of wok and add broccoli.

Cook until broccoli is tender and pork is fully cooked, about 10 minutes. Add peanuts and serve immediately.

MAKES 4 SERVINGS.

LAMB CHOPS WITH PEANUT SAUCE

1½ lb (750 g) lamb chops
2 Tbsp (30 ml) peanut oil
3 cloves garlic, chopped
6 Tbsp (90 ml) soy sauce
1 Tbsp (15 ml) dark molasses
½ cup (125 ml) homemade peanut butter
juice of 1 lemon
pinch salt
fresh ground pepper to taste

Broil lamb chops about 8 to 10 minutes a side, depending upon their thickness.

In a skillet heat oil and add garlic; sauté until soft.

Remove pan from heat and add soy sauce, molasses and peanut butter; stir until combined.

Return skillet to burner on medium heat.

Add lemon juice, salt and pepper to taste and cook about 2½ minutes.

Reduce heat to simmer and keep sauce warm until lamb chops are cooked.

Serve over lamb chops.

MAKES 4 SERVINGS.

PEANUT LOAF

⅔ cup (150 ml) cooked oatmeal (or rice)
¼ cup (50 ml) chopped green pepper
pinch salt
3 Tbsp (45 ml) minced onion
2 Tbsp (30 ml) lemon juice
1 cup (250 ml) chopped peanuts
⅔ cup (150 ml) dry bread crumbs
1 cup (250 ml) grated cheddar cheese
1 egg
⅓ cup (75 ml) milk

In a mixing bowl combine all ingredients.
Place in a greased 9 x 5 x 3-inch (23 x 13-cm) loaf pan.
Bake 1 hour at 350° F (180° C).

MAKES 6 SERVINGS.

NUT BURGERS

1 cup (250 ml) uncooked brown rice
4 cups (1 L) ground walnuts
1 cup (250 ml) shredded cheddar cheese
1 egg, slightly beaten
¼ cup (50 ml) minced onion
¼ tsp (1 ml) chili powder
salt, pepper to taste
flour
oil

Cook rice according to package directions; combine with nuts, cheese, egg, onion and seasonings.
Shape into patties and coat with flour.
In a skillet fry patties in oil until brown on both sides.

MAKES 6 BURGERS.

SATAY

1 Tbsp (15 ml) soy sauce
1 Tbsp (15 ml) oil
1 Tbsp (15 ml) lemon juice
1 garlic clove, minced
1 Tbsp (15 ml) peeled, grated ginger root
1 Tbsp (15 ml) brown sugar
10 oz (300 g) lean pork (or chicken), cubed
2 cups (500 ml) cooked rice

PEANUT SAUCE

¼ cup (50 ml) peanut butter
2 tsp (10 ml) soy sauce
3 Tbsp (45 ml) water
1½ tsp (7 ml) firmly packed brown sugar
⅛ tsp (.5 ml) cayenne pepper
⅛ tsp (.5 ml) sesame oil

Combine soy sauce, oil, lemon juice, garlic, ginger and brown sugar and stir well; add pork or chicken, coating well and refrigerate 2–3 hours.

Prepare rice according to package directions and keep warm.

Thread meat onto skewers and cook under the broiler or on the barbecue until done.

Make peanut sauce combining all ingredients; add more water if necessary; sauce should be consistency of pancake batter.

Place rice on serving dishes; ease meat off skewers onto rice and drizzle sauce over meat and rice.

MAKES 2 SERVINGS.

VEAL PISTACHIO

1 lb (500 g) veal scallops (thin, boneless pieces)
salt, pepper to taste
8 Tbsp (120 ml) butter, divided
1 cup (250 ml) orange juice
4 tsp (20 ml) lime juice
½ tsp (2 ml) grated orange peel
4 Tbsp (60 ml) toasted chopped pistachios

Lightly season veal with salt and pepper.

Using half the butter sauté veal 25 seconds a side; do not overcook; remove and keep warm.

Add juices and peel to skillet; reduce over high heat until mixture thickens.

Add pistachios; remove from heat and add remaining butter; mix until melted.

Arrange veal on a serving plate and pour sauce over veal.

MAKES 4 SERVINGS.

BLACK WALNUT MEATBALLS

1½ lbs (750 g) lean ground beef
1 cup (250 ml) chopped black walnuts
1 garlic clove, minced
1 cup (250 ml) dry bread crumbs
2 eggs
½ cup (125 ml) milk
salt, pepper to taste
2 Tbsp (30 ml) cooking oil
1 10-oz (284-ml) can condensed mushroom soup

In a mixing bowl combine beef, walnuts, garlic and bread crumbs.

In a separate bowl combine eggs, milk and seasonings; add to beef mixture and blend well.

Shape into balls.

In a skillet brown meatballs in oil.

Add mushroom soup and simmer for 20 minutes, until meat is tender.

Serve over noodles.

MAKES 6 SERVINGS.

Seafood Main Dishes

ALMOND SEAFOOD CASSEROLE

1 lb (500 g) cooked crabmeat, flaked
1½ cups (375 ml) cooked shrimp
1 cup (250 ml) mayonnaise
½ cup (125 ml) chopped onion
1 cup (250 ml) sliced mushrooms
1 8½-oz (240-g) can sliced water chestnuts, drained
2 cups (500 ml) diced celery
1 cup (250 ml) chopped green pepper
2 tsp (10 ml) Worcestershire sauce
½ tsp (2 ml) paprika
2 cups (500 ml) buttered croutons
¾ cup (175 ml) toasted slivered almonds
2 cups (500 ml) shredded cheddar cheese

In a large bowl combine crab meat, shrimp, mayonnaise, vegetables, and seasonings.

In a greased 9 x 13-inch (22 x 33-cm) pan arrange half the croutons.

Top with half the seafood mixture, half the almonds and half the cheese; repeat layering.

Bake 30 minutes at 375° F (190° C).

MAKES 8–10 SERVINGS.

TROUT ALMANDINE

¼ cup (50 ml) flour
1 tsp (5 ml) seasoned salt
1 tsp (5 ml) paprika
2 lbs (1 kg) trout fillets, skin on
¼ cup (50 ml) melted butter
½ cup (125 ml) sliced almonds
2 Tbsp (30 ml) lemon juice
5 drops hot pepper sauce
1 Tbsp (15 ml) fresh chopped parsley

Combine flour, salt, and paprika and use to coat both sides of trout. Place fillets in a well-greased baking dish, skin side down in a single layer.

Drizzle trout with 2 Tbsp (30 ml) of melted butter and broil for 10–15 minutes, until fish flakes easily.

While fish is broiling, sauté almonds in remaining butter, stirring constantly; remove from heat and stir in lemon juice, hot pepper sauce and parsley.

Pour over fish and serve immediately.

MAKES 6 SERVINGS.

THAI SALMON WITH ALMONDS

¼ cup (50 ml) sliced almonds
3 Tbsps (45 ml) butter, divided
¾ tsp (3 ml) ginger
1½ tsp (7 ml) jalapeno peppers, seeded and chopped
3 garlic cloves, chopped
⅛ cup (30 ml) soy sauce
⅛ cup (30 ml) brown sugar
¼ cup (50 ml) sweetened shredded coconut
¼ cup (50 ml) sliced green onion
¼ cup (50 ml) fresh chopped coriander
4 salmon steaks, each about 1-inch (2.5-cm) thick

Sauté almonds in half the butter; remove and set aside.

Stir-fry ginger, peppers, garlic, soy sauce, sugar, coconut and onion in remaining butter, about 1 minute; remove from heat and stir in coriander.

Grill salmon steaks until firm, 10–11 minutes; top with stir-fry mixture and sprinkle with almonds.

MAKES 4 SERVINGS.

ALMOND SALMON LOAF

1 1-lb (500-g) canned salmon, drained and flaked
2 green onions, chopped with greens
½ cup (125 ml) chopped green pepper
1 cup (250 ml) cooked mushrooms
2 Tbsp (30 ml) water
1 cup (250 ml) chopped almonds
2 eggs, lightly beaten
1 cup (250 ml) dry bread crumbs
salt, pepper to taste
milk

In a mixing bowl combine all ingredients well, adding milk if needed to bind mixture together.

Place in a greased 9 x 5 x 3-inch (22 x 13-cm) loaf pan.

Bake 40 minutes at 350° F (180° C).

MAKES 6 SERVINGS.

CASHEW HALIBUT

6 6-oz (170-g) halibut steaks
salt
butter
3 cups (750 ml) dry bread crumbs
⅓ cup (75 ml) finely chopped salted cashews
pepper to taste
6 Tbsp (90 ml) butter

Sprinkle both sides of fish with salt and arrange in a buttered baking dish.

Top each piece of fish with a pat of butter.

In a mixing bowl combine bread crumbs, cashews, pepper and butter.

Cover fish with crumb mixture.

Bake 35 minutes at 350° F (180° C) until crumbs are brown.

MAKES 6 SERVINGS.

COCONUT GROUPER

2 lbs (1 kg) grouper fillets
juice of 5 limes
5 garlic cloves, minced and divided
1 tsp (5 ml) salt
1 Tbsp (15 ml) oregano
2 coconuts, meat diced and juice reserved (or 2 cans unsweetened coconut milk)
1 Tbsp (15 ml) cooking oil
1 onion, chopped
1 green pepper, chopped
5 plum tomatoes
2 sprigs cilantro, chopped
2 chicken boullion cubes, crushed

Place fish in a glass baking dish.

Combine lime juice, 2 minced garlic cloves, salt and oregano and pour over fish.

Combine coconut meat and juice and set aside.

In a skillet heat oil and sauté onion, pepper and remaining garlic until soft; add tomatoes, cilantro and boullion cubes.

Simmer 5 minutes, then slowly add coconut mixture; stir and simmer 5 more minutes.

Remove fish from marinade and add to coconut mixture; simmer 10 minutes or until fish is cooked.

MAKES 4 SERVINGS.

COCONUT CURRIED SHRIMP

1 whole coconut in the shell
2 cups (500 ml) boiling water
¾ cup (175 ml) chopped green pepper
½ cup (125 ml) chopped onions
½ cup (125 ml) chopped almonds (or walnuts)
4 garlic cloves
2 tsp (10 ml) ground coriander
1 tsp (5 ml) salt
½ tsp (2 ml) turmeric
½ tsp (2 ml) cayenne pepper
⅓ cup (75 ml) peanut oil
1 bay leaf
1 Tbsp (15 ml) finely sliced ginger root
2 tsp (10 ml) grated lemon zest
1½ lb (750 g) raw shrimp (about 40) shells removed and deveined

Pierce the soft eye of the coconut and drain liquid (discard). Bake coconut 15 minutes at 400° F (200° C).

Break coconut with a hammer and remove meat from shell with a sharp knife. Place in a food processor with boiling water and blend until smooth.

Strain through a fine sieve and reserve liquid, about 1½ cups (375 ml).

Place vegetables, nuts and spices in food processor to make a fine paste.

In a large skillet heat peanut oil on high heat. Add nut paste, bay leaf, ginger, and lemon zest and sauté 3 minutes.

Add shrimp and sauté another 3 minutes. Add coconut milk and bring to a full boil; reduce heat and simmer 3 minutes.

Remove shrimp to a warm bowl with a slotted spoon. Increase heat and reduce sauce, stirring for 5 minutes, until thick. Remove bay leaf.

Pour sauce over shrimp and serve immediately.

MAKES 4 SERVINGS.

MACADAMIA-CRUSTED SNAPPER

olive oil
4 snapper fillets, 7–8 oz (200–250 g) each
¼ cup (50 ml) chardonnay wine
salt and pepper
1 cup (250 ml) toasted macadamias
½ cup (125 ml) heavy cream reduced by one third
2 Tbsp (30 ml) chopped parsley
2 Tbsp (30 ml) chopped basil
2 Tbsp (30 ml) chopped chives

¼ cup (50 ml) dry bread crumbs
2 Tbsp (30 ml) Parmesan cheese
2 Tbsp (30 ml) butter
2 Tbsp (30 ml) olive oil
2 Tbsp (30 ml) lemon juice

- Place fillets on a baking sheet and brush fish and sheet with olive oil.
- Pour chardonnay over each fillet and season with salt and pepper.
- Coarsely grind remaining ingredients in food processor and coat snapper fillets.
- Bake until flaky and moist, about 10 minutes, at 400° F (200° C).

MAKES 4 SERVINGS.

SAUCE

edible flowers (optional)
fresh basil to taste
¾ cup (175 ml) orange juice
1 Tbsp (15 ml) lemon juice
¼ cup (50 ml) chardonnay
½ tsp (2 ml) choppped garlic
1 tsp (5 ml) chopped shallots
2 Tbsp (30 ml) heavy cream
½–¾ lb (250–375 g) butter

- Slice edible flowers and basil into long ribbons.
- In a saucepan combine remaining ingredients except butter and reduce.
- Swirl in butter.
- Strain, then stir in flowers and basil.
- Serve immediately over snapper fillets.

MAKES 1¼ CUPS (375 ML).

Baked Goods, Desserts and Candy

Baked Goods, Desserts and Candy

Breads and Muffins

APRICOT ALMOND BREAD

1 cup (250 ml) dried apricots
1½ cups (375 ml) boiling water
2 Tbsp (30 ml) butter
1 cup (250 ml) sugar
1 tsp (5 ml) salt
1½ cups (375 ml) pastry flour
1 tsp (5 ml) baking soda
1 cup (250 ml) whole wheat flour
1 cup (250 ml) finely chopped almonds
1 egg, well beaten
1 tsp (5 ml) lemon or orange extract

In a food processor chop apricots ; add boiling water, butter, sugar and salt and mix well.

Sift pastry flour and baking soda and add to apricot mixture.

Add whole wheat flour, almonds, egg and extract; stir well.

Pour into a buttered loaf pan 9 x 5 x 3 inch (22 x 13 cm).

Bake 1¼ hours at 350° F (180° C), until knife inserted comes out clean. Cool in pan before cutting.

MAKES 1 LOAF.

ALMOND CRANBERRY MUFFINS

2¼ cups (550 ml) flour
¾ cup (175 ml) sugar
1½ tsp (7 ml) baking powder
⅜ tsp (1.5 ml) baking soda
pinch salt
3 large eggs
⅜ cup (75 ml) butter
¾ cup (175 ml) sour cream
¾ tsp (4 ml) almond extract
1⅛ cup (280 ml) sliced unblanched almonds
¾ cup (175 ml) whole-berry cranberry sauce

In a mixing bowl combine flour, sugar, baking powder, baking soda and salt and set aside.

In a separate bowl whisk eggs, butter, sour cream and almond extract; stir in ¾ cup (175 ml) of almonds.

Fold egg mixture into dry ingredients, stirring just enough to moisten batter.

Spoon 2 Tbsp (30 ml) of batter into each greased or paper-lined muffin cup.

Top each with 1 Tbsp (15 ml) of cranberry sauce.

Cover with remaining batter; sprinkle with almonds.

Bake 20 minutes at 375° F (190° C), until golden brown.

Let stand 20 minutes and remove muffins from cups.

MAKES 12 MUFFINS.

COCONUT CORNBREAD

1 cup (250 ml) yellow cornmeal
1 cup (250 ml) all-purpose flour
1 Tbsp (15 ml) sugar
1 Tbsp (15 ml) baking powder
1¼ tsp (6 ml) allspice
pinch salt
1 egg, beaten
1 cup (250 ml) mashed bananas
¼ cup (50 ml) milk
¼ cup (50 ml) oil
⅓ cup (75 ml) water (or coconut juice from fresh coconut)
½ cup (125 ml) sweetened flaked coconut (or fresh, flaked coconut)

In a mixing bowl combine cornmeal, flour, sugar, baking powder, allspice and salt.

In a separate bowl combine egg, bananas, milk, oil and water; mix well.

Combine wet and dry ingredients then fold in coconut.

Turn batter into a greased 8-inch (20-cm) square pan.

Bake 25–30 minutes at 375° F (190° C), until knife inserted comes out clean. Cool in pan before cutting.

MAKES 9 SQUARES.

PEANUT BUTTER MUFFINS

2 cups (500 ml) all-purpose flour
1 Tbsp (15 ml) baking powder
1 cup (250 ml) milk
2 eggs
½ cup (125 ml) sugar
½ cup (125 ml) creamy peanut butter
1 tsp (5 ml) salt

- In a mixing bowl combine flour and baking powder and set aside.
- In a blender or food processor combine milk, eggs, sugar, peanut butter and salt; add to dry ingredients, stirring just until moist.
- Spoon batter into greased or paper-lined muffin tins.
- Bake 15–20 minutes at 400° F (200° C).

MAKES 12 MUFFINS.

APPLE CHEDDAR PECAN BREAD

2½ cups (625 ml) all-purpose flour
½ cup (125 ml) sugar
2 tsp (10 ml) baking powder
1 tsp (5 ml) salt
½ tsp (2 ml) cinnamon
¾ cup (175 ml) milk
¼ cup (50 ml) margarine, melted
2 eggs
1½ cups (375 ml) shredded sharp cheddar cheese
1½ cups (375 ml) finely chopped peeled apples
¾ cup (175 ml) chopped pecans

- In a mixing bowl combine dry ingredients.
- In a separate bowl beat milk, margarine and eggs; add to dry ingredients, stirring just enough to moisten.
- Stir in cheese, apples and nuts just until blended.
- Turn batter into a greased and floured loaf pan 9 x 5 x 3 inch (22 x 13 cm).
- Bake 60–70 minutes at 350° F (180° C), until knife inserted comes out clean. Cool in pan before cutting.

LEMON WALNUT LOAF

½ cup (125 ml) shortening
1 cup (250 ml) sugar
2 eggs
1½ cups (375 ml) sifted all-purpose flour
pinch salt
1 tsp (5 ml) baking powder

½ cup (125 ml) milk
½ cup (125 ml) chopped walnuts
grated rind and juice of 1 lemon
¼ cup (50 ml) sugar

In a mixing bowl cream shortening and add sugar and eggs.
Add sifted flour, salt and baking powder alternately with milk.
Stir in nuts and lemon rind.
Turn into a greased loaf pan 8 x 4 x 3 inch (20 x 10 cm).
Bake 40 minutes at 350° F (180° C), until knife inserted comes out clean.
Dissolve sugar in lemon juice.
Remove loaf from oven and immediately brush with lemon mixture. Cool in pan before cutting.

MAKES 1 LOAF.

WALNUT DATE LOAF

1 cup (250 ml) chopped dates
½ tsp (2 ml) baking soda
¾ cup (175 ml) hot water or coffee
⅔ cup (150 ml) brown sugar
2 Tbsp (30 ml) butter
1 egg, beaten
1½ cups (375 ml) flour
1 tsp (5 ml) baking powder
½ tsp (2 ml) salt
¾ cup (175 ml) chopped walnuts

In a measuring cup place dates, soda and hot water.
Cool until lukewarm.
In a mixing bowl combine date mixture, sugar, butter and beaten egg.
Sift in dry ingredients and stir in nuts.
Turn batter into loaf pan 9 x 5 x 3 inch (22 x 13 cm).
Bake 45 minutes at 325° F (160° C), until a knife comes out clean. Cool in pan before cutting.

MAKES 1 LOAF.

Pies

Nuts added to pie crusts enhance the flavor of desserts. Simply sprinkle ¼ cup (50 ml) of ground or finely chopped, toasted nuts on the bottom and sides of a raw pastry shell, and press nuts into the pie crust with the back of a spoon. Bake or fill as usual.

For unfilled pie shells, place rolled dough in pie plate and prick generously with a fork, or weight the bottom with rice, beans or pie weights, to avoid uneven baking. Remove weights just prior to removing pie shell from the oven to ensure even browning.

Preheat oven to 425° F (220° C) and bake 12 to 15 minutes until lightly browned. Reduce baking time by 3 minutes if glass pie plate is used. Cool before filling.

ALMOND PASTRY

1 cup (250 ml) whole wheat pastry flour
½ cup (125 ml) all-purpose flour
½ tsp (2 ml) salt
½ tsp (2 ml) baking powder
2 Tbsp (30 ml) sugar
½ cup (125 ml) ground almonds
¼ cup (50 ml) vegetable shortening
¼ cup (50 ml) unsalted butter
2–3 Tbsp (30–45 ml) ice water

- In a mixing bowl sift dry ingredients together; add bran from flour left in sifter back into mixture.
- Mix in sugar and almonds.
- Cut in shortening and butter until dough is crumbly.
- Drizzle ice water over mixture, 1 Tbsp (15 ml) at a time; toss lightly until dough is moist enough to hold together, but not too sticky.
- Shape dough into a ball, wrap tightly in plastic wrap and refrigerate 30 minutes before rolling.

ENOUGH FOR 1 SINGLE CRUST.

NUT CRUMB CRUST

2 Tbsp (30 ml) melted butter
1 Tbsp (15 ml) sugar
¼ cup (50 ml) finely chopped nuts
⅔ cup (150 ml) graham cracker crumbs
¼ tsp (1 ml) nutmeg
¼ tsp (1 ml) cinnamon

- In a mixing bowl combine all ingredients.
- Spread evenly on the bottom of an 8-inch (20-cm) springform pan; press firmly and chill until filling.

ENOUGH FOR 1 SINGLE CRUST.

SWEET SHORTCRUST

¼ cup (50 ml) unsalted butter, softened
¼ cup (50 ml) superfine sugar
1 egg, beaten and liquid divided in half
1½ cups (375 ml) flour, sifted
1 Tbsp (30 ml) ground almonds

- In a food processor cream butter and sugar.
- Beat in half the egg mixture, then add flour and ground almonds.
- When dough begins to form a ball, wrap in plastic and chill 2 hours.
- Butter a 9-inch (22-cm) tart tin with a removeable collar.
- On a lightly floured surface, roll dough ⅛ inch (3 mm) thick.
- Line base and sides of tart tin, trimming excess.
- Line tart with baking parchment and baking beans.
- For a partially baked case, cook 15–20 minutes at 350° F (180° C), until shell begins to color.
- For a fully-cooked case, bake 25–30 minutes at 350° F (180° C).
- Cool and remove collar. Remove paper and beans before filling.

MAKES 1 SINGLE CRUST.

PLUM AND ALMOND TART

1 part-baked 9-inch (22-cm) sweet shortcrust
¾ cup (175 ml) whole blanched almonds
¼ cup (50 ml) unsalted butter, softened
⅓ cup (75 ml) superfine sugar
1 egg plus 1 egg white
14 oz (420 g) sweet, ripe purple plums (or apricots, etc.)
icing sugar

- In a food processor grind almonds until fine; add butter and sugar and combine well.
- Add egg and egg white and blend until smooth.
- Smooth mixture on cooked tart crust.
- Cut plums in half and place cut side up on the custard crust.
- Bake 45 minutes at 325° F (170° C) until custard is golden, risen and firm.
- Dust with icing sugar when cool.
- Serve at room temperature.

MAKES 6 SERVINGS.

ALMOND AMARETTO PIE

CRUST

2 cups (500 ml) finely shredded coconut
¾ cup (175 ml) semi-sweet chocolate chips
4 Tbsp (50 ml) unsalted butter
1½ tbsp (25 ml) light corn syrup

FILLING

¼ cup (50 ml) Amaretto liqueur
2 tsp (10 ml) unflavored gelatin
½ cup (125 ml) sour cream
1½ cups (375 ml) whipping cream
1 cup (250 ml) icing sugar
¾ cup (175 ml) finely chopped toasted almonds

- To make crust warm coconut in the oven at 250° F (120° C) without browning.
- In the top pan of a double boiler melt chocolate chips, butter and corn syrup together; stir until smooth.
- Mix in warm coconut and press into the bottom and sides of a 9-inch (22-cm) pie plate.
- To make filling combine Amaretto with gelatin in a heat resistant cup.
- Place cup in simmering water and heat until gelatin dissolves.
- Transfer gelatin to a large bowl and add sour cream; blend well.
- Whip cream until stiff peaks form; add icing sugar and ½ cup (125ml) almonds and spoon into pie shell.
- Garnish with remaining almonds and refrigerate 2 hours.

MAKES 8–10 SERVINGS.

BERRY TART

1 9-inch (22-cm) uncooked sweet shortcrust (see page 157)

ALMOND SPONGE

2 Tbsp plus 1 tsp (35 ml) unsalted butter
¼ cup (50 ml) superfine sugar
½ cup plus 1 Tbsp (140 ml) ground almonds
1 egg

- In a food processor cream butter and sugar; add almonds and egg and blend well.
- Spread on uncooked tart case.
- Bake 25 minutes at 350°F (180° C). Cool.

CREME MOUSSELINE

1 cup plus 2 Tbsp (280 ml) milk
¼ cup plus 1 Tbsp (65 ml) unsalted b
2 egg yolks
¼ cup (50 ml) superfine sugar
¼ cup plus 2 tsp (70 ml) flour
12–14 oz (340–400 g) fresh fruit (r
blackberries, kiwi, grapes cut in h
½ cup (125 ml) apricot jam

In a saucepan bring milk to a bo one quarter of the butter.

In a separate bowl whisk egg yo until pale, then whisk in flour.

Gradually whisk in milk, blend smooth.

Return mixture to saucepan a 2 minutes, stirring constantly. Re heat and cool.

In a food processor, beat ren until pale, then beat into cooled

Spread mixture onto the ba crust and chill 2 hours.

Arrange berries on top of c

Force jam through a sieve. lightly graze fruit, then chill ur

MAKES 6–8 SERVINGS.

ND LEMON PIE

2-cm) pie crust, baked and cooled
te

firmly packed brown sugar
5 ml) grated lemon rind
45 ml) lemon juice
ml) almond extract
45 ml) cream
(45 ml) whole wheat flour
(60 ml) unsalted butter, melted
175 ml) coarsely chopped toasted
nds
(30 ml) sliced almonds

a mixing bowl beat egg white, eggs and sugar until fluffy.

lend in lemon rind, juice, extract, cream, and butter.

old in chopped almonds.

our filling into prebaked crust; sprinkle sliced almonds.

Bake 30 minutes, until filling is set, at ° F (190° C).

KES 6–8 SERVINGS.

MACADAMIA PIE

1 9-inch (22-cm) unbaked pastry shell
3 eggs
⅔ cup (150 ml) sugar
1 cup (250 ml) light corn syrup
¼ cup (50 ml) butter, melted
1 tsp (5 ml) vanilla extract
1 cup (250 ml) chopped macadamias
whipped cream (or ice cream)

In a mixing bowl cream eggs, sugar, syrup, butter and vanilla.

Stir in nuts.

Turn mixture into an unbaked pastry shell.

Bake 40–45 minutes at 375° F (180° C).

Serve warm with whipped cream or ice cream.

MAKES 6–8 SERVINGS.

PEANUT BUTTER PIE

1 9-inch (22-cm) pie crust baked and cooled

CHOCOLATE FILLING

½ cup (125 ml) butter, softened
½ cup (125 ml) icing sugar
1 egg
¾ cup (175 ml) semi-sweet chocolate chips, melted
1 tsp (5 ml) vanilla extract
½ cup (125 ml) chopped peanuts

PEANUT BUTTER FILLING

8 oz (250 g) cream cheese, softened
½ cup (125 ml) creamy peanut butter
1 cup (250 ml) icing sugar
1 egg
1½ cups (375 ml) frozen whipped topping, thawed
¼ cup (50 ml) chopped peanuts

Make chocolate filling by creaming butter and icing sugar in a small bowl until fluffy.

Beat in egg for 2 minutes; blend in chocolate and vanilla and mix well.

Spread 1 cup (250 ml) of filling over cooled pie crust and sprinkle with ½ cup (125 ml) of chopped peanuts.

Make peanut butter filling by creaming peanut butter and cream cheese in a large mixing bowl. Add sugar and egg. Beat until creamy.

Fold in whipped topping.

Spoon peanut butter filling over chocolate filling.

Spread remaining chocolate filling over peanut butter filling, leaving a 2-inch (5-cm) border around the edge.

Sprinkle ¼ cup (50 ml) of chopped peanuts around the border.

Refrigerate 3 hours before serving.

MAKES 8–10 SERVINGS.

SAWDUST PIE

1 9-inch (22-cm) unbaked deep dish pie crust
7 egg whites, unbeaten
1½ cups (325 ml) sugar
1½ cups (325 ml) graham cracker crumbs
1½ cups (325 ml) pecans
1½ cups (325 ml) coconut
bananas
whipped cream

Combine egg whites, sugar, graham cracker crumbs, pecans and coconut, and stir by hand.
Pour into unbaked pie crust.
Bake 25–30 minutes, at 325° F (160° C) until crust is done.
Serve warm with sliced bananas and whipped cream.

MAKES 8–10 SERVINGS.

PECAN PIE

1 9-inch (22-cm) unbaked pie shell
3 eggs
½ cup (125 ml) firmly packed brown sugar
2 Tbsp (30 ml) flour
1½ cups (375 ml) dark corn syrup
1 tsp (5 ml) vanilla
pinch salt
1 cup (250 ml) pecans

In a mixing bowl beat egg until light; mix in sugar and flour and beat well.
Add syrup, vanilla, salt and pecans.
Pour into unbaked pie crust.
Bake 10 minutes at 425° F (220° C).
Reduce heat to 325° F (160° C) and continue to bake 45 minutes until brown.

MAKES 8–10 SERVINGS.

CRANBERRY PECAN PIE

1 9-inch (22-cm) unbaked pie crust
1 cup (250 ml) fresh cranberries
1 Tbsp (15 ml) plus 1 cup (250 ml) sugar
1 tsp (5 ml) plus 1 Tbsp (15 ml) grated orange zest
¾ cup (175 ml) dark corn syrup
½ cup (125 ml) butter
3 eggs, lightly beaten
2 Tbsp (30 ml) dark rum
½ tsp (2 ml) vanilla
¾ cup (175 ml) coarsely chopped pecans, lightly toasted

Bake pie crust for 10 minutes at 375° F (180° C) lined with aluminum foil and filled with pie weights.

Cut cranberries in half and stir in 1 Tbsp (15 ml) sugar and 1 tsp (5 ml) of orange zest; set aside.

In a saucepan combine remaining sugar and orange zest with corn syrup and butter; cover and cook over medium heat, stirring often, until sugar dissolves; bring to a boil and remove from heat.

In a mixing bowl whisk eggs, rum and vanilla; slowly pour ½ cup (125 ml) of hot syrup mixture into eggs; beat constantly so eggs don't cook.

Slowly add remaining syrup, stirring constantly and set aside.

Sprinkle cranberries and pecans over bottom of partially baked crust.

Pour syrup mixture over berries and pecans.

Bake 45 minutes to 1 hour at 375° F (190° C) until pie sets.

Cool and keep covered until serving.

MAKES 8–10 SERVINGS.

DEEP DISH DOUBLE CHOCOLATE CHIP AND BOURBON PECAN PIE

CRUST

2½ cups (625 ml) all-purpose flour
1 Tbsp (15 ml) sugar
8 ozs (250 g) cold unsalted butter, cut into small pieces
½ tsp (2 ml) salt
½-¾ cup (125 ml–175 ml) ice-cold milk

FILLING

6 whole eggs
7 egg yolks
8 oz (250 g) unsalted butter, melted
1 cup (250 ml) sugar
1¾ cups (425 ml) dark corn syrup
⅓ cup (75 ml) bourbon
1 cup (250 ml) semi-sweet chocolate chips
1 cup (250 ml) good quality white chocolate
1½ cups (375 ml) chopped pecans
½ cup (125 ml) whole pecan halves

To make crust combine flour, sugar, cold butter and salt in a food processor. Pulse 5–10 seconds until butter is the size of small peas.

Add ½ cup (125 ml) milk and pulse 3–4 times; if necessary add more milk, 1 Tbsp (15 ml) at a time until dough holds together.

Wrap dough in plastic wrap and flatten into a round disk; refrigerate 1 hour.

Butter a 9-inch (22-cm) springform pan, roll out dough and line pan, letting extra dough hang over sides.

To make filling combine all ingredients, except whole pecan halves, in a large mixing bowl, whisking until smooth; do not whip until foamy.

Pour mixture into chilled dough.

Decoratively place pecan halves on top.

Trim dough level with top of pan.

Cover pan with foil and bake on a baking sheet for 2 hours at 350° F (180° C) or until middle of pie is firm.

Cool and let pie set in refrigerator at least 4 hours.

Individual slices may be heated in a 350° F (180° C) oven for 10 minutes or until warm and served with ice cream.

MAKES 10–12 SERVINGS.

WALNUT FUDGE PIE

1 9-inch (22-cm) unbaked pie crust
3 eggs
¾ cup (175 ml) sugar
1 cup (250 ml) dark corn syrup
2 oz (60 g) milk chocolate
2 oz (60 g) unsweetened chocolate
1 Tbsp (15 ml) melted butter
1 tsp (5 ml) vanilla
¼ cup (50 ml) coffee
pinch salt
1½ cups (375 ml) coarsely chopped walnuts
whipped cream

In a mixing bowl beat eggs, sugar and corn syrup.

In a saucepan melt chocolates and butter and add to egg mixture.

Add vanilla, coffee and salt and stir until smooth.

Pour into unbaked pie crust and arrange walnuts on top.

Bake 5 minutes at 425° F (220° C); reduce heat to 350° F (180° C) and continue to bake 30–40 minutes.

Cool and serve at room temperature topped with whipped cream.

MAKES 8–10 SERVINGS.

MAPLE WALNUT PIE

1 9-inch (22-cm) pie crust made of almond pastry (see page 156) (may substitute walnuts for almonds)
4 eggs
¾ cup (175 ml) pure maple syrup
½ tsp (2 ml) vanilla
½ tsp (2 ml) cinnamon
pinch salt
grated rind of 1 orange
4 Tbsp (60 ml) unsalted butter, melted
2 Tbsp (30 ml) sour cream
2 cups (500 ml) toasted walnut pieces

In a mixing bowl combine all ingredients except walnut pieces and mix well.

Sprinkle walnuts over pastry shell.

Pour filling over walnuts.

Bake 10 minutes at 425° F (220° C); reduce temperature to 375° F (190° C) and bake until filling is set, 20–25 more minutes.

MAKES 8–10 SERVINGS.

Cakes

BASIC NUT CAKE

4 eggs
⅓ cup (75 ml) light brown sugar
1 tsp (5 ml) vanilla
pinch salt
⅓ cup (75 ml) white sugar
1 cup (250 ml) ground nuts (almonds, walnuts, hazelnuts, macadamias, pecans, or pistachios may be used)
½ cup (125 ml) all-purpose flour
4 Tbsp (60 ml) unsalted butter, melted and cooled

Separate 3 of the eggs, placing yolks and whites in separate bowls; add remaining egg to the yolks, beating at medium speed.

Add brown sugar and vanilla and beat on high about 3 minutes until mixture is light.

Add salt to the egg whites and beat at medium speed until soft peaks form; increase speed to high and add white sugar, beating until whites are glossy and hold firm peaks.

Using a spatula, fold whites into yolk mixture.

Fold nuts into egg mixture until half mixed.

Sift flour over the batter and continue to fold into the mixture until smooth. Keep batter light; do not over mix.

Fold melted butter into batter.

Place batter into a 9-inch (22-cm) round pan that has been buttered and the bottom lined with wax or parchment paper that has also been buttered.

Bake 25 minutes at 350° F (180° C), until golden.

Remove cake from pan and cool on a rack.

MAKES 9 SERVINGS.

CHOCOLATE ALMOND POUND CAKE

2½ cups (625 ml) all-purpose flour
⅔ cup (150 ml) cocoa
pinch salt
½ tsp (2 ml) baking powder
½ tsp (2 ml) baking soda
1 cup (250 ml) butter, softened
2½ cups (625 ml) sugar
6 eggs
1½ cups (375 ml) sour cream
½ tsp (2 ml) almond extract
½ cup (125 ml) toasted slivered almonds

In a small bowl combine flour, cocoa, salt, baking powder and baking soda and set aside.

In a mixing bowl cream butter about 2 minutes; add sugar and blend until creamy. If mixture becomes shiny it is over beaten. Refrigerate to chill butter.

Add eggs, one at a time, beating each well; beat in sour cream and almond extract.

Gradually blend in flour mixture.

Place toasted almonds into greased and floured 12-cup (3-L) tube pan; pour in batter and bake 70 minutes at 350° F (180° C).

Cool 15 minutes and remove from pan.

Cool completely before cutting.

MAKES 12–14 SERVINGS.

VIENNESE APPLE-ALMOND TORTE

BASE

½ cup (125 ml) butter
⅓ cup (75 ml) sugar
¼ tsp (1 ml) vanilla
1 cup (250 ml) flour
¼ cup (50 ml) raspberry jam

FILLING

8 oz (250 g) cream cheese
¼ cup (50 ml) sugar
1 egg
½ tsp (2 ml) vanilla

TOPPINGS

⅓ cup (75 ml) sugar
½ tsp (2 ml) cinnamon
4 cups (1 L) peeled, cored and sliced apples
½ cup (125 ml) sliced almonds

To make crust, cream butter, sugar and vanilla.
Blend in flour and press on bottom and sides of a 9-inch (22-cm) springform pan.
Spread with a thin layer of jam.
To make filling, combine cream cheese and sugar.
Add egg and vanilla and mix well.
Pour mixture over jam.
For the topping, toss apples with sugar and cinnamon and spoon over cream cheese mixture. Sprinkle top with almonds.
Bake for 10 minutes at 450° F (230° C). Reduce oven to 400° F (200° C) and continue baking 25 minutes.
Cool and carefully remove side of pan.
Store in a cool place or refrigerate until serving.

MAKES 8–10 SERVINGS.

BRAZIL NUT FRUIT CAKE

3 eggs
1 lb (500 g) whole pitted dates
½ lb (250 g) red glacé cherries
½ lb (250 g) green glacé cherries
1 lb (500 g) whole Brazil nuts
¾ cup (175 ml) sifted all-purpose flour
¾ cup (175 ml) sugar
½ tsp (2 ml) baking powder
½ tsp (2 ml) salt
1 tsp (5 ml) vanilla

In a mixing bowl beat eggs until light; add fruit and nuts.
Sift flour, sugar, baking powder and salt over fruit mixture.
Add vanilla and mix well.
Pour batter into a 9 x 5 x 3-inch (22 x 13-cm) loaf pan that has been lined with two layers of buttered, heavy brown paper.
Bake 1¾–2 hours at 300° F (150° C) with a pan of hot water on the rack below the cake.
Cool thoroughly before serving. Wrap in foil to store several weeks.

MAKES 12 SERVINGS.

APPLESAUCE PEANUT CAKE

¼ cup (50 ml) butter
½ cup (125 ml) peanut butter
1 cup (250 ml) sugar
1 egg
1¼ cups (300 ml) sifted all-purpose flour
1 tsp (5 ml) baking soda
1 tsp (5 ml) salt
½ tsp (2 ml) cinnamon
¼ tsp (1 ml) nutmeg
¼ tsp (1 ml) cloves
1 cup (250 ml) applesauce

In a mixing bowl cream butter, peanut butter and sugar.
Add egg and beat well.
In a separate bowl sift dry ingredients together.
Add to creamed mixture alternately, with applesauce.
Pour batter into a greased, wax-paper-lined 8-inch (20-cm) square cake pan.
Bake 40 minutes at 350° F (180° C). Turn out of pan and cool on wire rack.

MAKES 9 SERVINGS.

PEANUT TORTE

3 cups (750 ml) finely chopped roasted peanuts
2 Tbsp (30 ml) all-purpose flour
2 tsp (10 ml) baking powder
6 eggs, separated
1½ cups (375 ml) sugar, divided
1½ tsp (7 ml) vanilla
¼ tsp (1 ml) salt

FROSTING

½ cup (125 ml) icing sugar
2 cups (500 ml) whipping cream
½ cup (125 ml) grated chocolate
peanut halves

In a mixing bowl combine peanuts, flour and baking powder and set aside.
In a separate bowl beat egg yolks and 1 cup (250 ml) sugar until thick and light colored; add vanilla, then stir into peanut mixture.
In a separate bowl beat egg whites and salt until stiff; gradually add ½ cup (125 ml) sugar and fold into peanut mixture.
Pour batter into three 9-inch (22-cm) round cake pans that have been greased and lined on the bottom with wax paper.
Bake 30 minutes at 325° F (160° C).
Cool 15 minutes, loosen around edges and remove from pans to cool further on wire racks, removing wax paper.

To make frosting, combine icing sugar and whipping cream and beat until soft peaks form; chill.

When ready to serve spread whipped cream on each layer and sprinkle with grated chocolate; stack layers and garnish top with peanut halves.

MAKES 6–8 SERVINGS.

APPLE PECAN WALNUT CAKE

1½ cups (375 ml) vegetable oil
1½ cups (375 ml) white sugar
½ cup (125 ml) brown sugar
3 large eggs
1 Tbsp (15 ml) vanilla
3 cups (750 ml) all-purpose flour
1 Tbsp (15 ml) cinnamon
1 tsp (5 ml) nutmeg
1 tsp (5 ml) baking soda
½ tsp (2 ml) salt
4 cups (1 L) peeled diced apples
¾ cup (175 ml) chopped walnuts
¾ cup (175 ml) chopped pecans

TOPPING

4 Tbsp (60 ml) butter
4 Tbsp (60 ml) brown sugar
4 Tbsp (60 ml) white sugar
4 Tbsp (60 ml) whipping cream
1 tsp (5 ml) vanilla
¼ cup (50 ml) whole pecans

In a mixing bowl beat oil and sugars; beat in eggs one at a time; add vanilla.

In a separate bowl sift flour, spices, baking soda and salt; stir into batter.

Fold in apples and nuts.

Pour into a buttered and floured 10-inch (25-cm) tube pan.

Bake 2 hours at 325° F (160° C), until tester comes out clean.

Cool cake half an hour in the pan; then loosen edges with a knife and turn onto a wire rack to cool.

To make topping, combine all ingredients, except pecans, in a saucepan; bring to a boil, then pour over cake.

Decorate with whole pecans.

MAKES 12–16 SERVINGS.

WALNUT CAKE

1½ cups (375 ml) butter
2 cups (500 ml) sugar
6 egg yolks
¾ cup (175 ml) milk
¼ cup (50 ml) brandy

1 tsp (5 ml) vanilla
3½ cups (875 ml) flour
½ tsp (2 ml) salt
2 cups (500 ml) coarsely chopped walnuts
6 egg whites
1 tsp (5 ml) cream of tartar
icing sugar

In a mixing bowl cream butter and gradually add sugar, beating until fluffy; beat in egg yolks.

In a small bowl combine milk, brandy and vanilla; add to butter mixture.

In a separate bowl sift flour and salt; add walnuts and combine with milk mixture.

Beat egg whites until foamy and add cream of tartar. Beat until egg whites are stiff.

Fold into batter gently but thoroughly.

Pour batter into a greased and floured 8-inch (20-cm) tube pan.

Bake 2½ hours at 275° F (140° C).

Cool half an hour, then remove from pan.

Sift icing sugar over top of cake.

MAKES 10–12 SERVINGS.

PRINCESS ELIZABETH CAKE

1 cup (250 ml) boiling water
1 tsp (5 ml) baking soda
1 cup (250 ml) finely chopped dates
¼ cup (50 ml) butter
1 cup (250 ml) sugar
1 egg, beaten
1½ cups (375 ml) flour
1 tsp (5 ml) salt
1 tsp (5 ml) baking powder
1 tsp (5 ml) vanilla

ICING

4 Tbsp (60 ml) brown sugar
½ cup (125 ml) coconut
3 Tbsp (45 ml) butter
2 Tbsp (30 ml) cream or milk
½ cup (125 ml) walnuts

Pour boiling water over dates and soda and let stand.

In a mixing bowl cream butter and sugar; add beaten egg and mix.

Sift in flour, salt and baking powder.

Add date mixture and vanilla.

Turn batter into an 8-inch (20-cm) square pan.

Bake 25 minutes at 350° F (180° C).

To make icing, combine brown sugar, coconut, butter and cream in a saucepan and boil 3 minutes.

Add walnuts and pour over warm cake.

Brown cake lightly under the broiler before serving.

MAKES 10–12 SERVINGS.

Desserts

ALMOND CURRIED FRUIT

1 14-oz (400-ml) can pear halves
1 14-oz (400-ml) can peach halves
1 14-oz (400-ml) can apricot halves
1 14-oz (400-ml) can pineapple rings
4 oz (125 g) maraschino cherries
3 Tbsp (45 ml) butter
1 cup (250 ml) brown sugar
1 tsp (5 ml) curry powder
1 Tbsp (15 ml) cornstarch
2 Tbsp (30 ml) sherry
1 cup (250 ml) slivered toasted almonds

Drain fruit well and arrange in a 9 x13-inch (22 x 33-cm) casserole.
In a saucepan melt butter, add sugar, curry powder, cornstarch and sherry.
Pour over fruit; top with almonds.
Bake 40 minutes at 350° F (180° C) and serve hot.

MAKES 10–12 SERVINGS.

ALMOND MERINGUE

3 egg whites
1 cup (250 ml) sugar
1 cup (250 ml) finely chopped blanched slivered almonds

In the top pan of a double boiler combine egg whites and sugar; beat over hot water until stiff peaks form.
Remove from heat and fold in almonds.
Spoon into a heavily greased and floured 9-inch (22-cm) pie plate; smooth top.
Bake 1 hour at 275° F (140° C).
Cool, cut in wedges and serve with sauce or fruit.

MAKES 10–12 SERVINGS.

BLANCMANGE

½ lb (250 g) blanched almonds
½ cup (125 ml) milk
¼ cup (50 ml) water
1 Tbsp (15 ml) gelatin
¼ cup (50 ml) water
1 cup (250 ml) cream
½ cup (125 ml) sugar
1 Tbsp (15 ml) kirsch or orgeat syrup

Grind almonds in a food processor until fine; gradually add milk and ¼ cup (50 ml) water.

Strain mixture through cheese cloth; reserve liquid and discard almonds.

In a separate bowl soak gelatin in ¼ cup (50 ml) water.

In a saucepan heat cream and sugar until scalded.

Dissolve gelatin in hot cream mixture; stir in almond milk and kirsch.

Pour into individual custard cups; chill about 4 hours.

Serve with fruit or sauce.

MAKES 4–6 SERVINGS.

CHESTNUT FREEZE

4 egg yolks
¼ cup (50 ml) sugar
½ cup (125 ml) cream
¼ tsp (1 ml) mace
2 Tbsp (30 ml) rum or brandy
1 cup (250 ml) whipping cream, whipped
1 cup (250 ml) ground chestnuts
1 cup (250 ml) graham cracker crumbs

In a mixing bowl beat egg yolks with sugar, cream and mace and cook in the top pan of a double boiler for 5 minutes, stirring constantly until thickened.

Chill. Add rum and fold mixture into whipped cream.

Pour a ½ inch (1 cm) layer onto the bottom of a 9 x 13-inch (22 x 33-cm) pan.

Peel chestnuts and grind to a fine powder in a food processor.

Sprinkle with a layer of ground chestnuts and a layer of cracker crumbs; repeat until all ingredients are used.

Freeze until firm.

MAKES 30 SQUARES.

MARRONS GLACÉS

2 lbs (1 kg) chestnuts (about 34–50)
water
4 cups (1 L) sugar
1 lb (500 g) glucose or dextrose
7 drops vanilla

Cut a slash or X in the shell of each chestnut without piercing the nut meat; blanch in boiling water, several chestnuts at a time, for two minutes.

Remove with a slotted spoon, peel the shell and inner brown skin.

In a large pan of cold water, place chestnuts and simmer about 15 minutes; remove from heat and drain.

In a separate pan combine half the sugar with all of the glucose and 1½ cups (375 ml) of water; bring to a boil, add chestnuts; bring back to a boil, remove pan from heat, cover and leave overnight.

The next day, bring pan of chestnuts to a boil, remove from heat, cover and leave overnight.

On the third day, add vanilla and reheat for the last time; remove from heat and cool.

When chestnuts are somewhat cooled, lift out with a slotted spoon and drain on a wire rack for 2 hours.

In a saucepan, dissolve remaining sugar in 1 cup (250 ml) of water; bring to a boil to make a syrup.

Keep syrup hot over low heat.

Ladle some syrup into a small, warm bowl; dip chestnuts then remove to wire rack; as syrup becomes cloudy, discard it and replace with a fresh batch.

Dry marrons in a warm place, turning them after an hour and a half.

After three hours of drying, store in a covered container lined with wax paper.

MAKES ABOUT 50.

COCONUT RUM FLAN

2 14-oz (300-ml) cans sweetened condensed milk
4 eggs
½ cup (125 ml) shredded coconut
¼ cup (50 ml) dark rum

In a mixing bowl beat condensed milk and eggs until foamy and stir in coconut and rum.

Pour into a 9-inch (22-cm) round glass dish or pie plate.

Place dish in a pan of hot water so water comes halfway up the sides of the glass dish.

Bake 1 hour at 350° F (180° C).

Cool and unmold while still warm.

Serve warm or cold.

MAKES 6 SERVINGS.

HAZELNUT BAVARIAN CREAM

1 Tbsp (15 ml) gelatin
2 Tbsp (30 ml) cold water
½ cup (125 ml) milk
4 egg yolks
¼ cup (50 ml) sugar
pinch salt
¾ cup (175 ml) ground hazelnuts

1 tsp (5 ml) vanilla
2 cups (500 ml) whipping cream
chocolate sauce
hazelnuts

In a small dish soak gelatin in cold water.
In a saucepan scald milk.
Combine egg yolks, sugar and salt. Add a small amount of milk to egg yolk mixture, then gradually add egg yolk mixture to milk; stir well over low heat until thick.
Stir in gelatin mixture until dissolved and remove from heat.
Add hazelnuts and vanilla and cool.
Whip cream until stiff peaks form and fold in.
Pour pudding into a 9-inch (22-cm) serving dish or oiled mold and chill at least 12 hours.
Serve with chocolate sauce and garnish with hazelnuts.

MAKES 6 SERVINGS.

PECAN SOUFFLÉ

1⅓ cups (325 ml) toasted pecan pieces
3 large egg yolks
⅓ cup (75 ml) sugar
1 Tbsp (15 ml) all-purpose flour
1½ Tbsp (25 ml) cornstarch
1 cup (250 ml) milk
4 egg whites
2 Tbsp (30 ml) sugar
icing sugar

In a food processor chop toasted pecans until fine; set aside.
In a mixing bowl beat egg yolks, ⅓ cup (75 ml) sugar, flour and cornstarch until pale yellow and thick.
In a saucepan bring milk to a boil.
Whisk into egg mixture and return to the saucepan.
Heat, stirring constantly, until custard thickens.
Remove from heat and stir in pecans; set aside until cool.
Beat egg whites until soft peaks form; beat in 2 Tbsp (30 ml) of sugar and beat until stiff peaks form.
Stir a quarter of the egg whites into the pecan mixture to lighten it.
Fold in remaining egg whites in two stages.

Turn mixture into a buttered and sugared 8-inch (20-cm) soufflé dish or individual ramekins.

Bake 20–30 minutes at 375° F (190° C).

Dust with icing sugar and serve immediately

MAKES 4 SERVINGS.

PECAN BREAD PUDDING WITH RUM SAUCE

3 cups (750 ml) milk
3 eggs
2½ Tbsp (35 ml) butter, melted
1½ cups (375 ml) sugar
½ tsp (2 ml) cinnamon
½ tsp (2 ml) nutmeg
1½ Tbsp (25 ml) vanilla
4½ cups (1 L, 125 ml) stale bread, cubed
½ cup (125 ml) chopped pecans
¾ cup (175 ml) raisins, soaked overnight in water and drained

SAUCE

½ lb (250 g) butter
2 cups (500 ml) sugar
¼ cup (50 ml) rum
5 Tbsp (75 ml) cornstarch
4 Tbsp (60 ml) milk
2 egg yolks, beaten

To make pudding, combine milk, eggs and butter in a mixing bowl and beat until smooth and thick; beat in sugar, spices and vanilla.

Toss bread, pecans and raisins together.

Grease a 9-inch (22-cm) square pan and pack the bread mixture into the pan; pour milk mixture on top and let stand 45 minutes; flatten well.

Bake 45 minutes at 350° F (180° C), until firm.

To make sauce, melt butter in a saucepan over medium heat; stir in sugar and boil 7 or 8 minutes until golden.

Remove from heat and whisk in rum.

Dissolve cornstarch in milk and whisk into mixture.

Return to low heat and stir constantly until thick; remove from heat and let cool several minutes.

Whisk in beaten egg yolks with sauce.

Cut pudding and serve with sauce.

MAKES 10 SERVINGS.

Squares

ALMOND SQUARES

½ cup (125 ml) butter
1 cup (250 ml) sugar
2 egg yolks
1½ cups (375 ml) all-purpose flour
1 tsp (5 ml) baking powder
½ tsp (2 ml) almond extract
pinch salt

TOPPING

2 egg whites
1 cup (250 ml) brown sugar
1 cup (250 ml) minced blanched almonds

Cream butter and sugar.

Add egg yolks, flour, baking powder, almond extract and salt.

Mix well and pat into an 8-inch (20-cm) square pan.

Beat egg whites until stiff peaks form.

Fold in brown sugar and almonds.

Spread over crust.

Bake 45 minutes at 250° F (120° C) until topping is crisp and brown.

Cool completely and cut into squares. May be frozen.

MAKES 9 SQUARES.

HAZELNUT CREAM CHEESE BROWNIES

FILLING

4 oz (125 ml) cream cheese, room temperature
¼ cup (50 ml) granulated sugar
1 egg
2 tsp (10 ml) lemon juice
½ tsp (2 ml) vanilla
¼ cup (50 ml) hazelnuts, roasted and finely ground

With an electric mixer beat cream cheese and sugar until smooth. Beat in egg, lemon juice and vanilla.

Fold in hazelnuts.

Refrigerate while preparing brownie batter.

BROWNIE BATTER

1 cup (250 ml) semi-sweet chocolate morsels
¼ cup (50 ml) butter
¾ cup (175 ml) all-purpose white flour
2 Tbsp (30 ml) cocoa
½ tsp (2 ml) baking powder
¼ tsp (1 ml) salt
¾ cup (175 ml) sugar
2 eggs
1 tsp (5 ml) vanilla
½ cup (125 ml) hazelnuts, roasted and coarsely chopped
icing sugar
candy thermometer

In the top pan of a double boiler melt chocolate and butter.

Cool to 100–110° F (38–43° C).

In a small bowl sift flour, cocoa, baking powder and salt and set aside.

In a large mixing bowl cream sugar, eggs and vanilla until smooth and lemon colored, about 2 minutes.

Beat in melted chocolate and butter.

Add dry ingredients and beat until well mixed.

Fold in chopped hazelnuts.

Spread half the batter into a greased 8-inch (20-cm) square pan.

Pour filling over bottom layer.

Gently spread remaining brownie batter over cream cheese layer.

For a marbelized effect, pull a metal spatula through the batter.

Bake 40 minutes at 350° F (180° C). Do not overbake.

Cool and serve, dusted with icing sugar.

MAKES 9 SQUARES.

MACADAMIA COCONUT BARS

CRUST

1 cup (250 ml) sifted flour
½ cup (125 ml) butter

FILLING

2 eggs, slightly beaten
1½ cups (375 ml) firmly packed brown sugar
2 Tbsp (30 ml) flour
¼ tsp (1 ml) baking powder
1 tsp (5 ml) vanilla
½ cup (125 ml) shredded coconut
1 cup (250 ml) chopped macadamias

FROSTING

2 Tbsp (30 ml) butter, softened
2 cups (500 ml) icing sugar, sifted
2 Tbsp (30 ml) orange juice
½ cup (125 ml) chopped macadamias

Combine crust ingredients and press into a 9-inch (22-cm) square pan; bake 15 minutes at 375° F (190° C).

In a mixing bowl combine eggs, sugar, flour, baking powder and vanilla; stir in coconut and nuts.

Spread filling over crust and bake 20 minutes at 375° F (190° C). Cool before frosting.

In a small bowl combine butter and icing sugar; mix in juice and spread frosting over filling; sprinkle nuts on top.

MAKES 12 SQUARES.

PEANUT BUTTER BROWNIES

½ cup (125 ml) flour
¼ tsp (1 ml) salt
½ cup (125 ml) crunchy peanut butter
¼ cup (50 ml) butter
1 tsp (5 ml) vanilla
1 cup (250 ml) firmly packed brown sugar
2 eggs
1 cup (250 ml) chopped peanuts

Sift flour and salt and set aside.

Cream peanut butter, butter and vanilla; add sugar, blending well.

Add eggs, one at a time, beating well.

Blend in flour mixture; stir in peanuts.

Spread evenly in a greased 8-inch (20-cm) square pan.

Bake 30–35 minutes at 350° F (180° C).

Cool 5 minutes and cut into squares.

MAKES 9 SQUARES.

CHOCOLATE PECAN COCONUT SQUARES

FIRST LAYER

½ cup (125 ml) butter
¼ cup (50 ml) plus 1 Tbsp (15 ml) cocoa
¼ cup (50 ml) sugar
1 egg, slightly beaten
1 tsp (5 ml) vanilla
½ cup (125 ml) chopped pecans
1 cup (250 ml) flaked coconut
2 cups (500 ml) graham cracker crumbs

SECOND LAYER

½ cup (125 ml) butter
6 Tbsp (90 ml) milk
4 Tbsp (60 ml) vanilla instant pudding mix
4 cups (1 L) icing sugar

THIRD LAYER

1 lb (500 g) semi-sweet chocolate chips
1 Tbsp (15 ml) butter

In the top pan of a double boiler, cook butter, cocoa, sugar and egg until thick, stirring constantly. Remove from heat.

Add vanilla, pecans, coconut and graham cracker crumbs and press into a 9 x 13-inch (22 x 33-cm) pan; chill 15 minutes.

In a mixing bowl cream butter, milk and pudding mix. Add icing sugar and combine well; spread over first layer.

In a saucepan over low heat melt chocolate chips and butter; stir until smooth and spread over second layer.

Chill until completely set and cut into squares. May be frozen.

MAKES 30 SQUARES.

PECAN SQUARES

CRUST

⅔ cup (150 ml) icing sugar
2 cups (500 ml) all-purpose flour
1 cup (250 ml) butter

TOPPING

⅔ cup (150 ml) melted butter
½ cup (125 ml) honey
3 Tbsp (45 ml) heavy cream
½ cup (125 ml) brown sugar
3½ cups (875 ml) coarsely chopped pecans

Sift icing sugar and flour together and cut in butter until fine crumbs form.
Pat crust into a 9 x 13-inch (22 x 33-cm) greased pan.
Bake 20 minutes at 350° F (180° C).
Combine melted butter, honey, cream and brown sugar together; stir in pecans until well coated.
Spread mixture over crust and bake 25 minutes longer.
Cool before cutting into squares.

MAKES 30 SQUARES.

WALNUT SQUARES

CRUST

1 cup (250 ml) all-purpose flour
½ cup (125 ml) butter
½ cup (125 ml) brown sugar

TOPPING

2 eggs
1 cup (250 ml) brown sugar
2 Tbsp (30 ml) all-purpose flour
½ tsp (2 ml) baking powder
1 cup (250 ml) chopped walnuts
½ cup (125 ml) coconut
1 tsp (5 ml) vanilla

Mix ingredients for crust to make a crumbly dough.
Press into an 8-inch (20-cm) square pan.
Bake 10 minutes at 350° F (180° C).
Combine remaining ingredients.
Pour over crust.
Bake 20–25 minutes at 350° F (180° C) until lightly browned.
Cool and cut into squares.

MAKES 14 SQUARES.

CHOCOLATE WALNUT BROWNIES

1 cup (250 ml) shortening
1½ cups (375 ml) brown sugar
2 eggs
1⅛ cups (280 ml) flour
¾ tsp (3 ml) baking powder
¼ tsp (1 ml) salt
4½ Tbsp (65 ml) cocoa
¾ tsp (3 ml) vanilla
½–1 cup (125–250 ml) chopped walnuts

ICING

1½ cups (375 ml) icing sugar
2½ Tbsp (35 ml) cocoa
3 Tbsp (45 ml) butter
2½ Tbsp (35 ml) milk
pinch vanilla

- Melt shortening and remove from heat.
- Add remaining ingredients to shortening.
- Pour batter into a 9 x 13-inch (22 x 33-cm) pan.
- Bake 15 minutes at 400° F (200° C). Reduce heat to 350° F (160° C) and bake 5 minutes longer; remove from oven and cool.
- To make icing combine icing sugar and cocoa.
- Cream butter and add milk and icing sugar mixture.
- Add vanilla and stir.
- Frost when completely cool and cut into squares.

MAKES 30 SQUARES.

Cookies and Balls

AUNT EVA'S ALMOND SHORTBREAD

1 cup (250 ml) butter
⅓ cup (75 ml) extra fine sugar
2 cups (500 ml) pastry flour
¼ tsp (1 ml) salt
1 cup (250 ml) chopped almonds

- In a mixing bowl cream butter and sugar.
- Combine almonds with flour and salt.
- Add to butter mixture; knead until dough is formed.
- Shape into a roll and chill thoroughly.
- Slice and bake on a floured baking sheet, 10 minutes at 350° F (180° C).

MAKES 4 DOZEN COOKIES.

CHRISTMAS ALMOND COOKIES

2 cups (500 ml) butter
2 tsp (10 ml) vanilla
2 tsp (10 ml) almond extract
⅔ cup (150 ml) sugar
4 Tbsp (60 ml) cold water
4 cups (1 L) flour
2 cups (500 ml) ground almonds
red and green colored sugar

In a mixing bowl cream butter, vanilla and almond extract; add sugar and beat until smooth.

Blend in cold water and stir in flour, beating until smooth.

Add ground almonds and chill dough 1 hour.

Form into 1-inch (2.5-cm) balls and roll in colored sugar; flatten with the bottom of a glass dipped in sugar.

Bake 15 minutes at 325° F (160° C).

MAKES 6 DOZEN COOKIES.

ALMOND COCONUT MACAROONS

¼ cup (50 ml) sugar
¾ cup (175 ml) icing sugar
2 Tbsp (30 ml) cake flour
4 egg whites, beaten
⅔ cup (150 ml) ground blanched almonds
½ tsp (2 ml) vanilla
2¼ cups (550 ml) shredded coconut

Sift sugars and flour together.

In a separate bowl beat egg whites until foamy; add sugar mixture, 2 Tbsps (30 ml) at a time, beating well after each addition.

Fold in almonds, vanilla and coconut.

Drop batter from a teaspoon onto a baking sheet.

Bake 20–25 minutes at 325° F (160° C).

MAKES 4 DOZEN COOKIES.

BRAZIL NUT COOKIES

½ cup (125 ml) butter, melted
1 lb (500 g) brown sugar
2 eggs, well beaten
1¼ cup (300 ml) flour
2 tsp (10 ml) baking powder
1½ cups (375 ml) chopped Brazil nuts

In a mixing bowl beat butter and sugar; add eggs and beat well.

Sift flour and baking powder into butter mixture, then stir in nuts.

Drop batter from a teaspoon onto a greased baking sheet.

Bake 15 minutes at 325° F (160° C).

MAKES 4 DOZEN COOKIES.

CASHEW COOKIES

1 cup (250 ml) flour
1 tsp (5 ml) baking powder
¼ tsp (1 ml) salt
6 Tbsp (90 ml) butter
½ cup (125 ml) sugar
1 egg, well beaten
1 cup (250 ml) chopped cashews
1 tsp (5 ml) vanilla
¼ cup (50 ml) milk

Sift flour and add baking powder and salt and sift again; set aside.

In a mixing bowl, cream butter and sugar; add egg, half the nuts and vanilla and beat well.

Add flour mixture alternately with milk and mix completely.

Drop batter from a teaspoon on a greased baking sheet; sprinkle with remaining nuts.

Bake 8–10 minutes at 425° F (220° C) being careful not to burn.

MAKES 2 DOZEN COOKIES.

FLORENTINES

3 oz (85 g) finely chopped candied orange peel
¾ cup (175 ml) finely chopped blanched almonds
⅓ cup (75 ml) all-purpose flour
3 Tbsp (45 ml) unsalted butter
¾ cup (175 ml) heavy cream
½ cup (125 ml) sugar
2 Tbsp (30 ml) light corn syrup
½ tsp (2 ml) vanilla
candy thermometer

In a mixing bowl combine orange peel, almonds and flour; toss and set aside.

In a saucepan combine butter, cream, sugar and corn syrup; bring to a boil, stirring constantly and heat to 240° F (112° C).

Remove from heat and stir in vanilla and dry ingredients.

Line cookie sheets with parchment paper and drop batter by the heaping tablespoonful onto prepared sheets.

Bake 10–12 minutes until golden. Cool completely before removing from baking sheet.

Store between layers of wax paper in an airtight container.

MAKES 2½ DOZEN COOKIES.

HAZELNUT SANDWICH COOKIES

¾ cup (175 ml) unsalted butter
⅓ cup (75 ml) sugar
1½ cups (375 ml) all-purpose flour
1½ cups (375 ml) ground toasted hazelnuts
¼ tsp (1 ml) vanilla
⅛ tsp (.5 ml) salt
1 cup (250 ml) semi-sweet chocolate, finely chopped

Cream butter and sugar until fluffy; add flour, nuts, vanilla and salt and stir just until mixed.

Roll dough into a ball and cut in half; flatten each half, wrap in plastic and refrigerate until firm.

Roll dough between sheets of wax paper to a thickness of ⅛ inch (3 mm).

Cut dough into rounds with a cookie cutter.

Bake 10 minutes at 350° F (180° C) on baking sheets lined with parchment paper; cool completely on baking sheet.

Melt chocolate in the top pan of a double boiler.

Spread chocolate on flat side of cookie and top with flat side of another cookie; drizzle chocolate over tops of each sandwich.

Let chocolate set at room temperature.

MAKES 2 DOZEN COOKIES.

GERMAN HAZELNUT SPICE COOKIES

4 cups (1 L) sifted flour
2 tsp (10 ml) baking powder
1 cup (250 ml) sugar
½ tsp (2 ml) coriander
1 tsp (5 ml) cinnamon
1 tsp (5 ml) cloves
½ tsp (2 ml) nutmeg
¼ tsp (1 ml) cardamon
1 egg
2 tsp (10 ml) vanilla
3 Tbsp (45 ml) milk

¾ cup (175 ml) butter
½ cup (125 ml) ground hazelnuts

In a mixing bowl sift flour and baking powder.

Add sugar, spices, egg, vanilla and milk.

Stir well and cut in butter.

Add nuts and more flour if dough is not manageable.

Form dough into a ball and refrigerate at least 2 hours.

Turn onto a lightly floured board and roll ⅛ inch (3 mm) in thickness.

Cut into shapes and bake 7–8 minutes on a greased cookie sheet at 400° F (200° C).

MAKES 5 DOZEN COOKIES.

HAZELNUT BISCOTTI

1½ cups (375 ml) hazelnuts, toasted and skins removed
4 cups (1 L) all-purpose flour
½ tsp (2 ml) salt
1 tsp (5 ml) baking soda
¾ cup (175 ml) butter, softened
1½ cups (375 ml) sugar
4 large eggs slightly beaten
2 Tbsp (30 ml) Frangelico liqueur

Grind ½ cup (125 ml) of nuts very fine. Chop remainder very coarse.

In a mixing bowl combine all ingredients except coarse nuts, using an electric mixer on low speed. Stir in coarse nuts by hand.

Divide dough into 4 pieces. Roll each piece 1½ inches (4 cm) wide. Flatten tops slightly and place on a greased baking sheet.

Bake 15 minutes at 350° F (180° C) until tops are firm.

Remove from oven and cool 10 minutes.

With a sharp knife, cut dough into diagonal slices about ½ inch (1.2 cm) thick.

Arrange slices, cut side down, on baking sheet and bake another 15 minutes, until lightly browned on both sides. Cool.

MAKES ABOUT 4 DOZEN COOKIES.

MACADAMIA COOKIES

2 cups (500 ml) shortening
1 tsp (5 ml) vanilla
¾ cup (175 ml) brown sugar
¾ cup (175 ml) white sugar
2 eggs
2¾ cups (675 ml) flour
1 tsp (5 ml) salt
1 tsp (5 ml) baking soda
2 cups (500 ml) chopped macadamias
⅓ cup (75 ml) macadamias, halved

Cream shortening, vanilla and sugars until creamy; add eggs and beat well.

In a separate bowl combine flour, salt and soda; stir in chopped nuts.

Drop batter by the spoonful on baking sheet. Press half a macadamia into each cookie and bake 10 minutes at 350° F (180° C).

MAKES 8 DOZEN COOKIES.

MACADAMIA CHOCOLATE CHIP COOKIES

2¼ cups (550 ml) flour
1 tsp (5 ml) baking soda
½ tsp (2 ml) salt
1 cup (250 ml) margarine
¾ cup (175 ml) sugar
¾ cup (175 ml) firmly packed brown sugar
2 eggs
1½ tsp (7 ml) vanilla extract
2 cups (500 ml) semi-sweet chocolate chips
¾ cup (175 ml) chopped macadamias
½ cup (125 ml) flaked coconut

In a mixing bowl sift flour, baking soda and salt and set aside.

In a separate bowl cream margarine, sugars and egg until fluffy; stir in vanilla.

Add dry ingredients; stir in chocolate chips, nuts and coconut.

Drop batter by the ¼ cupful (50 ml) onto baking sheets.

Bake 16–19 minutes, until golden brown, at 375° F (190° C).

MAKES 2 DOZEN VERY LARGE COOKIES.

PECAN DATE COOKIES

6 Tbsp (90 ml) butter
1 cup (250 ml) sugar
2 large eggs
1 cup (250 ml) all-purpose flour
½ cup (125 ml) semi-sweet chocolate, melted
1 tsp (5 ml) vanilla
1 cup (250 ml) finely chopped dates
1 cup (250 ml) pecan pieces
pecan halves

In a mixing bowl cream butter and sugar; add eggs, flour, melted chocolate, vanilla, dates and pecan pieces.

Chill dough 1 hour.

Drop batter from a teaspoon onto a greased baking sheet; top each with a pecan half and bake 12 minutes at 375° F (190° C).

MAKES 3 DOZEN COOKIES.

PEANUT BUTTER OATMEAL COOKIES

3 cups (750 ml) flour
1 Tbsp (15 ml) baking soda
1½ tsp (7 ml) salt
1½ cups (375 ml) quick-cooking rolled oats
1½ cups (375 ml) white sugar
1½ cups (375 ml) brown sugar
1½ cups (375 ml) margarine
1½ cups (375 ml) peanut butter
1½ tsp (7 ml) vanilla
3 eggs
2 cups (500 ml) semi-sweet chocolate chips
1 cup (250 ml) chopped peanuts

In a mixing bowl sift flour, baking soda and salt; stir in rolled oats and set aside.

Cream sugars, margarine and peanut butter; add vanilla and eggs and beat well.

Add sifted ingredients and combine well.

Stir in chocolate chips and nuts and chill 2 hours.

Form dough into walnut-sized balls and place on a baking sheet.

Bake 10–12 minutes at 375° F (190° C).

MAKES 5 DOZEN COOKIES.

MEXICAN WEDDING COOKIES

1½ cups (375 ml) coarsely chopped pecans
1½ cups (375 ml) unsalted butter, softened
¼ tsp (1 ml) salt
⅔ cup (150 ml) icing sugar
2 tsp (10 ml) vanilla
3 cups (750 ml) all-purpose flour
icing sugar

Toast pecans for 8 minutes at 325° F (160° C); cool completely then grind to a powder.
In a large mixing bowl cream butter and salt until fluffy.
Add icing sugar and vanilla, beating until smooth.
Beat in pecans, then flour.
Roll dough into 1¼-inch (3-cm) balls and flatten.
Bake on greased baking sheet 10–12 minutes at 325° F (160° C); cookies will be pale in the center and brown on the edges.
Let stand 5 minutes then remove to cooling rack.
Sift icing sugar over cookies and let cool completely.
Store in airtight container.

MAKES 4 DOZEN COOKIES.

PINE NUT COOKIES

4 eggs
1½ cups (375 ml) sugar
½ tsp (2 ml) lemon zest
⅛ tsp (.5 ml) anise extract
2¼ cups (550 ml) sifted all-purpose flour
pinch salt
12 oz (360 g) pine nuts
⅓ cup (75 ml) icing sugar

In the top pan of a double boiler combine eggs and sugar.
Beat with an electric mixer at medium speed until mixture is lukewarm.
Remove from hot water and continue beating until thick and cool.
Beat in lemon zest and anise.
Stir in flour and salt; add more flour if dough is too sticky to work.
Drop batter from teaspoon onto lightly greased baking sheet; sprinkle with pine nuts and press lightly into dough.
Let stand 5 minutes, then bake 10–15 minutes at 375° F (180° C).
Cool on wire rack and sift icing sugar over tops.

MAKES 5 DOZEN COOKIES.

PISTACHIO COOKIES

2 cups (500 ml) all-purpose flour
1½ tsp (7 ml) baking powder
½ tsp (2 ml) salt
⅔ cup (150 ml) butter
1 cup (20 ml) sugar
1 egg
1 tsp (5 ml) vanilla
½ tsp (2 ml) almond extract
½ cup (125 ml) shelled chopped pistachio nuts

In a mixing bowl combine flour, baking powder and salt; sift and set aside.

In a separate bowl cream butter, sugar, egg, vanilla, and almond extract until fluffy.

Stir in nuts.

Form dough into a roll 1 inch (2.5 cm) in diameter, cover with plastic and chill.

Slice cookies ⅛-inch (3-mm) thick.

Place on a baking sheet and bake 8–10 minutes at 375° F (190° C).

MAKES 3 DOZEN COOKIES.

PISTACHIO SHORTBREAD

3 oz (85 g) shelled pistachio nuts
¼ cup (50 ml) sugar
1⅛ cups (280 ml) flour
¼ tsp (1 ml) baking powder
½ cup (125 ml) butter

Toast pistachios under the broiler, turning several times, until brown; cool and grind fine with the sugar.

In a mixing bowl sift flour and baking powder; add nut mixture and butter, working to a stiff dough.

Roll dough on a floured surface to ½ inch (1 cm) thick and cut into rounds.

Bake 35 to 40 minutes at 325° F (160° C).

MAKES 2 DOZEN COOKIES.

BLACK WALNUT COOKIES

1½ cups (375 ml) butter, softened
⅔ cup (150 ml) sugar
3 eggs
3 cups (750 ml) all-purpose flour
¼ tsp (1 ml) salt
½ tsp (2 ml) vanilla
⅔ cup (150 ml) finely chopped black walnuts

- In a mixing bowl cream butter and sugar until fluffy.
- Mix in eggs one at a time, beating well after each.
- Sift in flour and salt; add vanilla.
- Wrap dough in wax paper and refrigerate at least 4 hours.
- Roll dough to ⅜-inch (9-mm) thick.
- Cut with a 1-inch (2.5-cm) diameter cookie cutter and place on an ungreased cookie sheet.
- Sprinkle with black walnuts and chill 45 minutes.
- Bake 10 minutes at 325° F (160° C).
- Cool on rack.

MAKES 5 DOZEN COOKIES.

CHOCOLATE ALMOND BALLS

1 cup (250 ml) peanut butter
1 cup (250 ml) icing sugar
1 Tbsp (15 ml) butter
½ cup (125 ml) chopped dates
½ cup (125 ml) chopped cherries
½ cup (125 ml) slivered almonds
½ cup (125 ml) semi-sweet chocolate, melted

- In a mixing bowl cream peanut butter, icing sugar and butter.
- Stir in fruits and nuts and shape into bite-size balls; chill.
- Dip balls into melted chocolate and refrigerate until serving.

MAKES 3 DOZEN BALLS.

CINNAMON PECAN BALLS

1 cup (250 ml) margarine
2 cups (500 ml) sugar
2 eggs
2½ cups (625 ml) sifted flour
pinch salt
2 tsp (10 ml) baking powder
2 tsp (10 ml) vanilla
1 cup (250 ml) finely chopped pecans
4 tsp (20 ml) cinnamon

- Cream margarine and sugar until fluffy; add eggs and beat well.
- Sift in flour, salt and baking powder to egg mixture.
- Stir in vanilla and mix well.
- Chill dough 2 hours.
- In a separate bowl combine nuts and cinnamon.

Roll dough into bite-sized balls and roll in nut mixture.
Bake 8 minutes on greased baking sheet at 375° F (190° C).
Cool on wire rack.

MAKES 3 DOZEN BALLS.

RUM BALLS

2 cups (500 ml) vanilla wafer crumbs
1 cup (250 ml) icing sugar
¾ cup (175 ml) finely chopped pecans
2 Tbsp (30 ml) cocoa
2 Tbsp (30 ml) corn syrup
⅓ cup (75 ml) rum
icing sugar

In a mixing bowl combine all ingredients thoroughly.
Shape into bite-size balls and roll in icing sugar.
Refrigerate and store 2 days before serving for enhanced flavor.

MAKES 4 DOZEN BALLS.

PINE NUT SHORTBREAD BALLS

1 cup (250 ml) butter
1 cup (250 ml) icing sugar, divided
2 tsp (10 ml) vanilla
2 tsp (10 ml) anise seed
2 cups (500 ml) all-purpose flour
1 cup (250 ml) pine nuts

In a mixing bowl cream butter, ⅓ cup (75 ml) icing sugar, vanilla and anise seed.
Mix in flour and pine nuts.
Shape dough into bite-size balls.
Bake 35 minutes, until golden, at 275° F (140° C).
Sift remaining icing sugar over balls while still warm.

MAKES 3 DOZEN BALLS.

CANDY

Weather and altitude affect candy making: humid days call for longer cooking times and temperatures 2 degrees higher than on dry days, while some types of candies, like nougats and hard candies, must only be made on dry days.

Select cookware with a heavy bottom to prevent burning, and with a capacity to hold four times the volume of ingredients so candy won't boil over. For personal safety, use wooden utensils that can tolerate high heats for extended periods of time.

TEMPERATURES AND TESTS FOR SYRUP AND CANDIES

TEST	DESCRIPTION
THREAD	syrup spins a 2-inch (5 cm) thread when dropped from a fork or spoon (230°–234° F; 110°–112° C)
SOFT BALL	syrup when dropped into very cold water forms a soft ball that flattens on removal from water (234°–240° F; 112°–116° C)
FIRM BALL	syrup when dropped into very cold water forms a firm ball that does not flatten on removal from water (242°–248° F; 117°–120° C)
HARD BALL	syrup when dropped into very cold water forms a ball that is hard enough to hold its shape, yet pliable (250°–268° F; 121°–131° C)
SOFT CRACK	syrup when dropped into very cold water separates into threads that are pliable and not brittle (270°–290° F; 132°–143° C)
HARD CRACK	syrup when dropped into very cold water separates into threads that are hard and brittle (300°–310° F; 149°–154° C)
CLEAR LIQUID	sugar melts (320° F; 160° C)
BROWN LIQUID	liquid becomes brown (338° F; 170° C)

Candy

CHOCOLATE NUT FINGERS

¼ cup (50 ml) finely chopped mixed candied peel
⅓ cup (75 ml) coarsely chopped raisins
½ cup (125 ml) chopped almonds
2 Tbsp (30 ml) chopped walnuts
⅔ cup (150 ml) shredded coconut
2 Tbsp (30 ml) minced preserved ginger
1 Tbsp (15ml) sugar
13 ozs (370 g) semi-sweet chocolate
½ cup (125 ml) dark rum
icing sugar

- In a mixing bowl combine fruits, nuts, ginger and sugar and set aside.
- In the top pan of a double boiler melt 5 oz (140 g) chocolate.
- Add chocolate to fruit and nut mixture; add rum and let cool slightly.
- Dust surface with icing sugar and shape mixture into finger-sized logs; refrigerate until firm.
- Melt remaining chocolate; cool slightly and dip fingers in chocolate, covering thoroughly.
- Place on wax paper and allow to set at room temperature.
- Wrap in plastic and refrigerate.

MAKES 2 DOZEN.

ALMOND PECAN POPCORN CRUNCH

1 cup (250 ml) unpopped popcorn
1 tsp (5 ml) salt
1 lb (500 g) unsalted butter
1 cup (250 ml) white sugar
1 cup (250 ml) brown sugar
½ cup (125 ml) corn syrup
⅓ cup (75 ml) water
2 cups (500 ml) unblanched almonds
2 cups (500 ml) pecans
candy thermometer

- Pop corn and sprinkle with salt.
- In a saucepan melt butter and add sugars, corn syrup and water; bring to a boil stirring constantly.
- Insert candy thermometer and cook, stirring continuously until temperature reaches 295° F (146° C).
- Remove from heat and pour immediately over popcorn.
- Stir in nuts and toss like a salad, using two spoons, until the popcorn is well coated.
- Spread out on cookie sheets to harden.
- Cool, then store in airtight containers.

MAKES 3 LB (1.5 KG).

ALMOND BUTTER CRUNCH

2⅔ cups (650 ml) blanched whole almonds
6 oz (170 g) semi-sweet chocolate
6 oz (170 g) unsweetened chocolate
1 lb (500 g) butter
2 cups (500 ml) sugar
2 Tbsp (30 ml) corn syrup
pinch baking soda
candy thermometer

Split almonds in half and place on a buttered pan at 350° F (180° C) until crisp and light brown; cool.

In the top pan of a double boiler melt chocolates.

In a saucepan melt butter and sugar over low heat; add butter and corn syrup; insert candy thermometer.

Increase heat to bring mixture to a boil, stirring occasionally, until candy reaches 300° F (149° C) (hard crack stage).

Remove from heat and add baking soda (mixture may foam).

Spread cooled nuts on a clean pan; cover with butter mixture and let harden.

Spread half the melted chocolate over the top and let harden.

When cool, turn candy over and place on wax paper; spread with remaining chocolate.

Cool and break into pieces. Store in airtight containers.

MAKES 3 LBS (1.5 KG).

NOUGAT

1 cup (250 ml) sugar
½ cup (125 ml) water
3 Tbsp (45 ml) light corn syrup
½ tsp (2 ml) salt
2 egg whites, room temperature
½ cup (125 ml) honey
2½ cups (625 ml) blanched slivered almonds
½ cup (125 ml) blanched pistachios
1 tsp (5 ml) vanilla
candy thermometer

In a large saucepan combine sugar, water, half the corn syrup and salt; cook, stirring constantly until the sugar dissolves.

Insert candy thermometer and continue to cook until temperature reaches 290° F (143° C) (softest crack stage); remove from heat.

In a mixing bowl beat egg whites until stiff, not dry; add cooked syrup gradually, beating all the time.

In a saucepan boil honey and remaining corn syrup to 290° F (143° C) (soft crack stage); gradually add to the egg white mixture, beating constantly; add nuts.

Stand the bowl of nougat on a rack in a pan of water and steam, stirring occasionally, about 1½ hours.

When the nougat, cooled, is not sticky to the touch, add the vanilla.

Line an 11 x 8-inch (28 x 20-cm) pan with parchment paper.

Turn nougat into pan and cover with parchment paper.

Place a pan of the same size on top of the nougat and press with a heavy weight.

Let stand overnight.

Turn candy out of the pan and cut into bars.

Wrap candy in wax paper and store in an airtight container in a cool place.

MAKES 2 LBS (1 KG).

MARZIPAN

½ cup (125 ml) finely ground blanched almonds
½ cup (125 ml) sugar
1 egg white, beaten to form soft peaks
1 cup (250 ml) sifted icing sugar
lemon juice

In a mixing bowl combine almonds and sugar to form a soft paste.

Blend with fluffy egg white.

Add icing sugar to make a smooth paste.

Add lemon by the drop until dough is easy to handle.

Knead until smooth and form into various shapes.

Marzipan may be colored, dipped in chocolate, nuts, seeds, or fruit. Wrap in foil and store in a cool place.

MAKES ABOUT ½ LB (250 G).

BRAZIL NUT FUDGE

¾ cup (175 ml) evaporated milk
1 cup (250 ml) marshmallow cream
¼ cup (50 ml) butter
1½ cups (375 ml) sugar
¼ tsp (1 ml) salt
2 cups (500 ml) semi-sweet chocolate chips
1 tsp (5 ml) vanilla
1 cup (250 ml) chopped Brazil nuts

- In a saucepan combine milk, marshmallow cream, butter, sugar and salt and bring to a boil, stirring constantly.
- Boil 5 minutes over moderate heat.
- Remove from heat and add chocolate chips and vanilla; stir until smooth.
- Add nuts and pour into a greased 8-inch (20-cm) square pan.
- Chill until firm. Refrigerate to store.

MAKES 28 SQUARES.

COCONUT DREAMS

1½ cups (375 ml) sugar
½ cup (125 ml) milk
2 tsp (10 ml) butter
⅓ cup (75 ml) shredded coconut
⅓ cup (75 ml) chopped nuts
candy thermometer

- In a saucepan combine sugar and milk and cook until temperature reaches (234° F; 112° C) (soft ball stage).
- Add butter and coconut and stir until creamy.
- Add nuts and drop from a teaspoon on wax paper.
- Refrigerate until serving.

MAKES 3 DOZEN.

NEVER-FAIL PEANUT BRITTLE

3 cups (750 ml) sugar
1 cup (250 ml) white corn syrup
½ cup (125 ml) water
3 cups (750 ml) raw Spanish peanuts
1 Tbsp (15 ml) butter
1 tsp (5 ml) salt
2 tsp (10 ml) baking soda
candy thermometer

In a large saucepan boil sugar, corn syrup and water.

Insert candy thermometer and continue to boil until syrup reaches (300° F; 150° C) (hard crack stage).

Add peanuts and stir continuously.

Continue to cook until candy turns brownish gold.

Remove from heat and add butter, salt and baking soda.

Pour candy onto a buttered pan.

Cool and break into pieces. Store in airtight containers.

MAKES 3 LBS (1.5 KG).

PEANUT BUTTER CUPS

1 cup (250 ml) margarine
1½ cups (375 ml) smooth peanut butter
1½ cups (375 ml) graham cracker crumbs
2 cups (500 ml) icing sugar
1 cup (250 ml) semi-sweet chocolate chips
½ cup (125 ml) chopped roasted peanuts

In a saucepan melt margarine; stir in peanut butter, cracker crumbs and sugar and mix well.

Press into small muffin tins with paper liners (about 2 Tbsp (30 ml) each).

In the top pan of a double boiler melt chocolate; spread on top of crumb crust.

Sprinkle with peanuts and allow to set 1 hour before serving. Store in airtight containers in the refrigerator.

MAKES 2 DOZEN.

PEANUT BUTTER TRUFFLES

3 oz (85 g) semi-sweet chocolate
½ cup (125 ml) peanut butter
¼ cup (50 ml) icing sugar
¼ cup (50 ml) ground almonds
1 Tbsp (15 ml) cream
2 oz (55 g) semi-sweet chocolate
½ cup (125 ml) icing sugar

In the top pan of a double boiler melt 3 oz (85 g) chocolate; stir in peanut butter, ¼ cup (50 ml) icing sugar, almonds and cream.

Shape into bite-size balls and dip in remaining 2 oz (55 g) of melted chocolate; cool and roll in icing sugar.

Refrigerate to store.

MAKES 2 DOZEN.

PEANUT BUTTER FUDGE

1 cup (250 ml) brown sugar
½ cup (125 ml) white sugar
½ cup (125 ml) milk
½ tsp (2 ml) vanilla
½ cup (125 ml) chunky peanut butter
candy thermometer

In a saucepan combine sugars and milk and cook to 234° F (112° C) (soft ball stage).

Remove from heat and add vanilla and peanut butter and beat thoroughly.

Turn into a greased 8-inch (20-cm) square pan and cool. Refrigerate to store.

MAKES 28 SQUARES.

PRALINES

3 cups (750 ml) sugar
1 cup (250 ml) milk
1½ cups (375 ml) pecans
pinch salt
2 Tbsp (30 ml) butter
candy thermometer

In a saucepan, caramelize 1 cup (250 ml) of sugar (stirring constantly on low heat, 8–10 minutes, until sugar is melted and straw-colored).

In a separate saucepan, at the same time, bring to a boil 2 cups (500 ml) of sugar, milk, pecans, salt and butter.

Add boiling mixture to sugar, stirring vigorously.

Heat to 234° F (112° C) (soft ball stage).

Remove from heat and beat mixture until it thickens and looks shiny.

Drop by the teaspoonful on wax paper.

Cool. Wrap in foil and store in airtight containers.

MAKES 3 DOZEN.

PECAN TOFFEE

½ cup (125 ml) pecan pieces
1½ cups (375 ml) lightly packed brown sugar
½ lb (250 g) butter
3 oz (85 g) semi-sweet chocolate, chopped

Butter a 9-inch (22-cm) square pan; spread pecans on bottom.

In a saucepan combine sugar and butter; cook over medium heat, stirring constantly, for exactly 12 minutes from the time the butter melts. (Mixture should be bubbly.)

Pour mixture quickly over the nuts.

Place chocolate squares on top, immediately, to melt; spread evenly over top as it melts.

Cool and break into pieces. Wrap in foil and store in airtight containers.

MAKES 1 LB (500 G).

PINE NUT PRALINES

1 tsp (5 ml) baking soda
1 cup (250 ml) buttermilk
3 cups (750 ml) sugar
4 Tbsp (60 ml) butter
1 tsp (5 ml) vanilla
2 cups (500 ml) pine nuts
candy thermometer

In a large saucepan dissolve baking soda in buttermilk; stir in sugar and cook over medium heat to 234° F (112° C) (soft ball stage).

Remove from heat and add butter, vanilla and nuts.

Cool until you can comfortably hold your hand on the bottom of the pot.

Beat by hand with a wooden spoon until the mixture loses its gloss.

Drop onto wax paper by the heaping tablespoonful. Wrap in foil and store in airtight containers.

MAKES 4 DOZEN.

PENUCHE

1¾ cups (425 ml) firmly packed light brown sugar
1 Tbsp (15 ml) corn syrup
pinch salt
¾ cup (175 ml) evaporated milk
¼ cup (50 ml) water
1 Tbsp (15 ml) butter
1 tsp (5 ml) vanilla
⅔ cup (150 ml) chopped walnuts

In a saucepan, combine the first six ingredients, stirring constantly and cook to 234° F (112° C) (soft ball stage).

Allow to cool, then beat until smooth and creamy.

Stir in vanilla and nuts.

Turn into a buttered 8-inch (20-cm) square pan and smooth the surface.

Cut into squares and allow to set in pan. Wrap in foil and store in airtight containers.

MAKES 28 SQUARES.

CHOCOLATE WALNUT FUDGE

3 oz (85 g) unsweetened chocolate
1 cup (250 ml) lightly packed light brown sugar
1 cup (250 ml) white sugar
2 Tbsp (30 ml) light corn syrup
⅔ cup (150 ml) heavy cream
pinch salt
¼ cup (50 ml) butter
½ cup (125 ml) black walnuts
1 tsp (5 ml) vanilla
1 Tbsp (15 ml) brandy or rum
candy thermometer

In a large saucepan combine chocolate, sugars, syrup, cream and salt and bring to a boil.

Without stirring, cook to 234° F (112° C) (soft ball stage).

Remove from heat and cool to lukewarm; do not stir.

When cool, beat in butter, nuts and flavorings.

Beat until the candy thickens, about 3 minutes.

Turn into an 8-inch (20-cm) square pan and cut into squares before fudge hardens. Refrigerate to store.

MAKES 28 SQUARES.

Sauces and Frostings

NESSELROD SAUCE

1 lb (500 g) fresh chestnuts
4 cups (1 L) water
1½ cups (375 ml) sugar
1 Tbsp (15 ml) lemon juice
½ vanilla bean (or 1/4 tsp (2 ml) vanilla)
½ cup (125 ml) light corn syrup
¼ cup (50 ml) dark rum
¼ cup (50 ml) sugar
¼ cup (50 ml) golden raisins
¼ cup (50 ml) currants
¼ cup (50 ml) muscat raisins
½ cup (125 ml) coarsely diced candied cherries
¼ cup (50 ml) finely diced candied citron
2 Tbsp (30 ml) finely chopped candied orange peel
⅓ cup (75 ml) maraschino liqueur

Cut chestnuts in half; place in a saucepan and cover with water; boil 3 minutes and remove with a slotted spoon; peel shells and skin.

In a saucepan combine 4 cups (1 L) water, sugar, lemon juice and vanilla bean and bring the mixture to a boil; boil 3 minutes.

Lower heat and add chestnuts; simmer uncovered until chestnuts are transparent, about 30 minutes. (Syrup will be thick).

- Add corn syrup, mix and set aside.
- Mix rum and sugar together and set aside.
- In a saucepan, combine raisins and currants; add water to cover and bring to a boil; remove from heat and drain.
- Place fruit in a bowl, add sweetened rum and mix well; let stand, covered for 2 hours or overnight.
- In a separate bowl, combine remaining fruit with maraschino liqueur; cover and let stand 2 hours or overnight.
- Remove vanilla bean from syrup; may be wrapped and stored for future use.
- Remove about ⅓ of the chestnuts, mash and return to syrup.
- Combine bowls of fruit with chestnuts and mix well.
- Pour sauce into sterilized jars and store, refrigerated, at least 2 weeks.
- Always stir sauce before use.

MAKES ABOUT 4 PINTS.

COCONUT CREAM

1 cup (250 ml) heavy cream
¼ cup (50 ml) fresh grated coconut
1 Tbsp (15 ml) plus 2 tsp (10 ml) sugar
pinch salt
¾ tsp (3 ml) gelatin
1 Tbsp (15 ml) buttermilk

- In the top pan of a double boiler stir in cream, coconut, sugar and salt; simmer about 20 minutes.
- Dissolve gelatin in buttermilk.
- Stir in the cream and cool mixture over ice water.
- Stir as the mixture begins to thicken, then beat vigorously until small peaks form.

MAKES 2 CUPS (500 ML).

PEANUT BUTTER SAUCE

1 14-oz (420-ml) can sweetened condensed milk
⅓ cup (75 ml) peanut butter
chopped peanuts

- In a saucepan over low heat combine milk and peanut butter.
- Heat, stirring continuously, until well blended.
- Remove from heat and stir in peanuts.
- Serve warm or cold.

MAKES 1½ CUPS (375 ML).

COFFEE HAZELNUT SAUCE

1½ cups (375 ml) water
1 cup (250 ml) light corn syrup
3 Tbsp (45 ml) cornstarch
1 Tbsp (15 ml) instant coffee
2 Tbsp (30 ml) butter
1 tsp (5 ml) vanilla
½ cup (125 ml) chopped hazelnuts

In a saucepan combine water and corn syrup.

In a small bowl combine cornstarch and coffee; moisten with some of syrup mixture then stir into syrup mixture.

Cook and stir until sauce thickens and boils.

Remove from heat; add butter, vanilla and hazelnuts.

Cool slightly before using.

MAKES 2½ CUPS (625 ML).

CARAMEL SAUCE

1 cup (250 ml) sugar
pinch salt
½ cup (125 ml) water
¾ cup (175 ml) heavy cream
2 Tbsp (30 ml) butter
½ cup (125 ml) chopped toasted pecans
1 tsp (5 ml) rum

In a saucepan caramelize sugar to a rich amber color.

Remove from heat and carefully add salt, water and cream.

Bring back to a gentle boil and cook 15 minutes, stirring until the caramel is completely dissolved.

Remove from heat and stir in butter, pecans and rum.

MAKES 2 CUPS (500 ML).

CHOCOLATE PECAN SAUCE

4 oz (125 g) semi-sweet chocolate
1 cup (250 ml) cocoa
1 cup (250 ml) butter
¼ cup (50 ml) boiling water
2 cups (500 ml) icing sugar
boiling water
1 cup (250 ml) sugar
1 cup (250 ml) whole pecans

In the top pan of a double boiler melt chocolate, cocoa and butter.

Stir in water to thin sauce.

Stir in icing sugar to create a thick sauce; adjust water or icing sugar so sauce is thick.

In a saucepan caramelize sugar stirring constantly on low heat, 8–10 minutes until sugar is melted and straw-colored. Add to sauce and combine thoroughly.

Remove from heat and stir in pecans.

Pour into sterilized jars to store at room temperature.

MAKES 3 CUPS (750 ML).

PECAN BOURBON SAUCE

4 cups (1 L) whipping cream
½ cup (125 ml) butter
½ cup (125 ml) brown sugar
1 Tbsp (15 ml) vanilla
4 Tbsp (60 ml) bourbon
¼ cup (50 ml) pecans

In a small saucepan combine all ingredients and heat over medium heat until blended.

Keep warm until serving.

MAKES 4 CUPS (1 L).

MARZIPAN FROSTING

1 cup (250 ml) blanched and unblanched almonds
4 cups (1 L) icing sugar
3 egg whites
1 tsp (5 ml) almond extract

In an electric blender or food processor grind almonds with icing sugar to a paste.

In a separate bowl beat egg whites to soft peaks and add to almond mixture.

Mix in extract.

MAKES 4 CUPS (1L).

MAPLE SYRUP ICING

1½ cups (375 ml) maple syrup
½ cup (125 ml) chopped nuts
candy thermometer

In a saucepan heat syrup until temperature reaches 234° F (112° C) (soft ball stage).

Without stirring cool to 110° F (43° C).

Beat until thick enough to spread.

Fold in nuts. If mixture becomes too hard, soften with a few drops of milk.

MAKES 1¾ CUPS (475 ML).

Almond Paste Icing

1 cup (250 ml) icing sugar
1 cup (250 ml) fine sugar
2 cups (500 ml) finely chopped blanched almonds
½ tsp (5 ml) lemon juice
½ tsp (2 ml) almond extract
3 egg yolks, beaten
egg white, slightly beaten

In a mixing bowl sift sugars and stir in almonds.

In a separate bowl combine juice, extract and beaten egg yolks. Add sugar mixture, egg white and combine to the consistency of bread dough.

Add more lemon juice if too crumbly, or icing sugar if too runny.

Knead, on a board sprinkled with icing sugar, until smooth.

Roll icing between two pieces of waxed paper until thin.

Place the cake carefully on top of the icing and trim the paste to fit the cake. Turn cake right side up.

Paste may be frozen for later use.

Clubs, Organizations and Mail Order Sources

ADULT PEANUT BUTTER LOVERS' FAN CLUB

P.O. Box 7528
Tifton, GA 31793
404-933-0357
FAX 404-933-0796

This organization celebrates peanut butter for adults. The club has more than 60,000 members from around the world, with honorary celebrity members including Bill Clinton, Chris Evert, Julia Child, Julia Roberts and Barbara Walters. The $3.00 membership includes a membership card and a one-year subscription to *Spread the News*, the official fan club newsletter. The club holds a convention every two years, attracting more than 1,000 people, with proceeds going to charity.

HAZELNUT MARKETING BOARD

P.O. Box 23126
Portland, OR 97281
503-639-3118
FAX 503-620-9808
800-503-NUTS

The Hazelnut Marketing Board represents all the hazelnut growers and handlers in Oregon where 99 percent of all U.S. hazelnuts are grown. The board established quality and volume regulations, production and marketing research, development projects and marketing promotions. They publish a quarterly, *The Inside Scoop*.

PEANUT BUTTER AND NUT PROCESSORS ASSOCIATION

9005 Congressional Court
Potomac, MD 20854
301-365-2521
FAX 301-365-7705

This is the national trade association of processors of peanut and tree nut products. The association represents the mutual business interests of nut processors with the media, the public and the U.S. federal government. They sponsor an annual convention.

Mail Order Sources

NUTS

ALMOND PLAZA

1701 C Street
P.O. Box 1768
Sacramento, CA 95814
916-446-2500
FAX 916-446-8532
800-225-6887

The Almond Plaza, owned by Blue Diamond, specializes in every kind of almond. They sell almond paste and almond oil, cashews, hazelnuts, pecans, pistachios, macadamias, mixed nuts, nut butters, and gift pack combinations. They also carry other products including smoked meats, olives, biscuits and preserves. They sell the almond cookbook, *New Almond Cookery*.

BYRD'S HOOT OWL PECAN RANCH

Route 3, Box 196
Butler, MO 64730
816-679-5583
816-925-3253

Loyle and Mary Byrd, proprietors

The Byrds' family-owned and -operated business began with 10 acres and 60 native pecan trees in 1958. The original farm is a 160-acre grove and processing plant near Butler. They also have a 219-acre (89 hectare) grove farther south near Nevada. Today, the trees number around 9,000, with 5,000 grafted trees and 4,000 native pecans. The store is open every day from November to January and their mail order business operates year-round.

PRODUCT LINE: *pecans, Missouri black walnuts.*

CHESTNUT HILL ORCHARDS, INC.

3300 Bee Cave Road
Suite 650
Austin, TX 78746-6663
512-477-3020
FAX 512-477-5551
800-745-3279

Michael Kelley, President

Chestnut Hill Orchards sells marrone quality chestnuts imported from northern Italy. These chestnuts, which are certified organically-grown, are steam-peeled and fresh-frozen, and are indistinguishable from raw chestnuts. They also sell chestnut flour. Chestnut Hill Orchards primarily sells in bulk to restaurants, restaurant distributors and manufacturers; however, they will also fulfill mail order requests from individuals.

PRODUCT LINE: *whole marrone chestnuts, steam-peeled and frozen; marrone chestnut pieces, steam-peeled and frozen; unsweetened marrone purée, frozen; chestnut flour; dried chestnuts, dehydrated and peeled.*

HAWAIIAN MACADAMIA PLANTATIONS, INC.

P.O. Box 707,
Honokaa, HI 96727
808-775-7201
800-444-6887

PRODUCT LINE: *macadamias (cocktail and snack, chopped and ground for cooking), chocolate-coated macadamias in white or dark chocolate, coconut chips, coffee, jams and jellies, brittle assortments, gift packs and gift baskets.*

KERNAL PEANUTS

R.R. #1
Vittoria, Ont. N0E 1W0
519-426-9222
FAX 519-426-9229

Nancy and Ernie Racz, owners

The Racz family began growing peanuts in 1982 and opened a wholesale and retail operation on their farm the same year. They welcome pre-arranged tours, best in mid to late summer when the plants are growing or during the fall harvest.

PRODUCT LINE: *roasted salted, unsalted and garlic-flavored peanuts in bags from 4 oz to 22 pounds (100 g to 10 kg); peanut butter (crunchy or smooth) by the jar or pail; peanut candies; custom ordered gift baskets.*

LUKE'S ALMOND ACRES

11281 South Lac Jac
Reedley, CA 93654
209-638-3483

Lucas and Barbara Nersesians, proprietors

The Nersesians sell home-grown almonds from their 20-acre (8-hectare) farm, in addition to a variety of dried fruit, nut and candied products. They operate a country store for their products and sell gift packs to stores like Macy's, in addition to mail-order. They send out a price list every October with fixed prices for the year.

PRODUCT LINE: *almonds, cashews, peanuts, pecans, pistachios, dried fruits, chocolate-covered and yogurt-covered treats, almond butter and gift box combinations.*

The Maples Fruit Farm

P.O. Box 167
Chewsville, MD 21721
301-733-0777
800-783-6888

The Maples Fruit Farm has been under family ownership for over 200 years. They offer nuts and dried fruits by the wholesale case, which range from 25 to 100 pounds (11 to 45 kg), depending upon the type of product, in addition to small-quantity orders.

Product line: *roasted (salted and unsalted) and raw nuts, dried fruit, fruit and nut mixes, gourmet gift baskets, maple syrup, chocolate-covered nuts, jelly beans, teas and coffees.*

Missouri Dandy Pantry

212 Hammons Drive
Stockton, MO 65785
417-276-5151
800-872-6879

Donna Hammons, proprietor

The pantry is run by Donna Hammons, daughter-in-law of Ralph Hammon, founder of Hammons Product Company, which is the world's largest processor of American black walnuts.

Product line: *Missouri black walnuts, Missouri pecans, nut candy, gift packs of nuts and candy, free brochure of black walnut recipes.*

Northwest Chestnuts

183 Shady Grove
Onalaska, WA 98570
360-985-7033

Annie and Omroa Bhagwandin, proprietors

Botanist Omroa Bhagwandin offers one-year-old chestnut seedlings that are open-pollinated, European or European X Chinese hybrids, adapted for the northwestern climate. Omroa will assist others with the set-up of their chestnut orchards and the marketing of their crops.

Annie Bhagwandin is the author and illustrator of *The Chestnut Cookbook*, which contains 90 recipes using chestnuts, practical information and folklore.

Product line: *chestnut flour, dried chestnuts, fresh chestnuts in season and The Chestnut Cookbook.*

Picard Peanuts

R.R. #1
Windham Centre, Ont. N0E 2A0
519-426-6700
FAX 519-443-7779

This is the site of the first commerical peanut shelling plant in Canada and home of the unique Canadian snack, the chipnut, a peanut covered in a crisp potato shell. There is a retail store at the plant and in the town of St. Jacobs. Tours by arrangement.

PRODUCT LINE: *peanuts; chipnuts; imported nuts; candy; baking products; dried fruit; party supplies.*

SQUIRE'S CHOICE

2250 W. Cabot Boulevard,
Langhorne, PA 19047
FAX 215-741-1799
800-523-6163

Squire's Choice began from the small town of Yardley, Pennsylvania, in an old carriage house. They are dedicated to providing the largest and most flawless nuts available anywhere in the world.

PRODUCT LINE: *almonds, cashews, macadamias, peanuts, pecans, pine nuts, pistachios, mixed nuts, dried fruit, candied nuts, and decorative gift box combinations. They offer a large variety of additional products including chocolate and candy, pecan pie, cookies, cheesecakes, and coffees.*

NUT CRACKERS

KINETIC KRACKER

P.O. Box 29153
Dallas, TX 75229-0153

The Kinetic Kracker offers several models of electric nut crackers for pecans and other thin-shelled nuts. Machines automatically adjust to the length and size of the nuts and come with a warranty.

NUT TREES

CAMPBERRY FARM

R.R. 1
Niagara-on-the-Lake, Ont.
LOS IJO
905-262-4927

R.D. Campbell, proprietor

Campberry Farm specializes in northern-hardy nut trees, including the black walnut, English walnut, American chestnut, Amercian hazel, shagbark hickory and northern pecan. Campberry provides consultation and site inspection services for growers interested in commercial nut tree production and discounts for those buying in hundred or thousand lot quantities. Pickups and visits are by appointment only. A catalogue is available.

CHESTNUT HILL NURSERY, INC.

Route I, Box 341
Alachua, FL
32615
904-462-2820
FAX 904-462-4330

R.D. Wallace, President

This nursery and orchard supplies trees budded onto Dunstan Chestnut or Chinese chestnut rootstocks. The Dunstan Chestnut is a blight-resistant tree with a combination of American and Chinese traits. It was developed from an American chestnut tree discovered in Ohio in the early 1950s. Dunstan Chestnuts were the first to receive a U.S. Plant Patent.

Chestnut Hill nursery offers orchard planting services, irrigation set up and management for new and existing orchards. They also offer contracts to purchase nut production from Dunstan chestnuts.

They publish *The Chestnut Grower*, a semi-annual journal devoted entirely to chestnuts.

Mellingers Inc.

Horticultural Merchants
2310 W. South Range Rd.
North Lima, OH 44452-9731
216-549-9861
FAX 216-549-3716

Product line: *Hall's hardy almond, black walnut, English walnut, Chinese chestnut, sweet hart chestnut, butternut, American hazelnut, European filbert, filazel, pecan, hickory, Turkish tree hazel.*

Associations

CANADA

The Northern Nut Growers Association

c/o R.D. Campbell
R.R. 1
Niagara-on-the-Lake, Ont.
LOS IJO

This association welcomes professional and amateurs dedicated to nut culture in colder climates. Membership includes a newsletter, meetings and a variety of projects and expeditions.

Society of Ontario Nut Growers

c/o R.D. Campbell
R.R. 1
Niagara-on-the-Lake, Ont.
LOS IJO

SONG encourages the planting of nut trees in Ontario. They publish a newsletter twice a year and hold special events.

Approximate Equivalents

ALMONDS

sliced	1 cup = 3 oz (85 g)
slivered	1 cup = 3¾ oz (105 g)
whole, blanched	1 cup = 5 oz (140 g)
whole, skins on	1 cup = 4 ½ oz (155 g)

BRAZIL NUTS

whole, skins on	1 cup = 4¾ oz (160 g)

CASHEW NUTS

whole, roasted	1 cup = 4¾ oz (160 g)

COCONUT

flaked	1 cup = 2¾ oz (75 g)
shredded	1 cup = 3½ oz (100 g)
dessicated	1 cup = 3 oz (85 g)

HAZELNUTS

whole, skins on	1 cup = 4 oz (125 g)

MACADAMIAS

whole	1 cup = 4½ oz (140 g)

PEANUTS

whole, blanched, roasted	1 cup = 4¾ oz (145 g)

PECANS

whole, toasted	1 cup = 4 oz (125 g)

PINE NUTS

whole, raw	1 cup = 4½ oz (140 g)

PISTACHIOS

whole, shelled	1 cup = 4 oz (125 g)

WALNUTS

whole, raw	1 cup = 4 oz (125 g)

Index

INDEX TO NUTS AND MAIL ORDER SOURCES

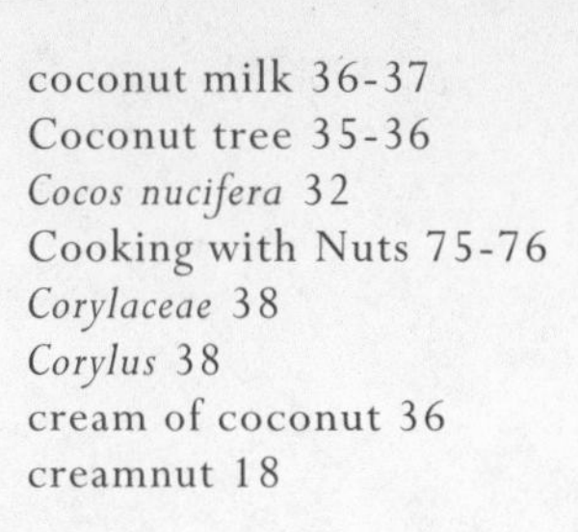

P

Q

R

S

T

W

INDEX TO RECIPES

A

D

E

F

G

H

I

L

M

R

S